Fantastic Feline Friends

Follow me on Facebook: Adult Coloring Books by L. Oliver
https://www.facebook.com/coloringbooksbyliz

Please share your works in progress and finished pages with me.
I love to see photos of your cats helping you color!

Relax, have fun, enjoy!

For use with markers I suggest putting a layer of cardstock below the page
to help prevent bleeding.

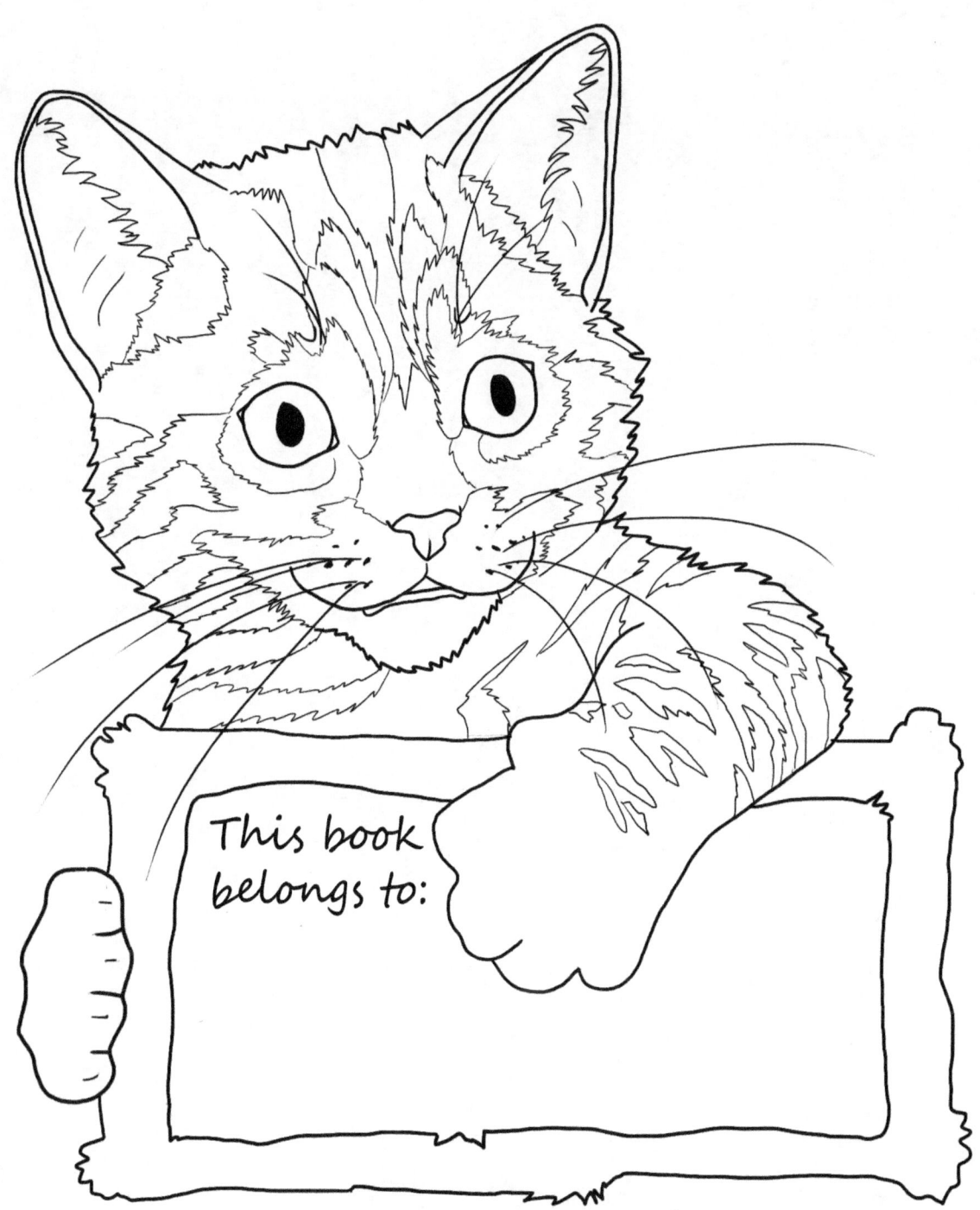

This book
belongs to:

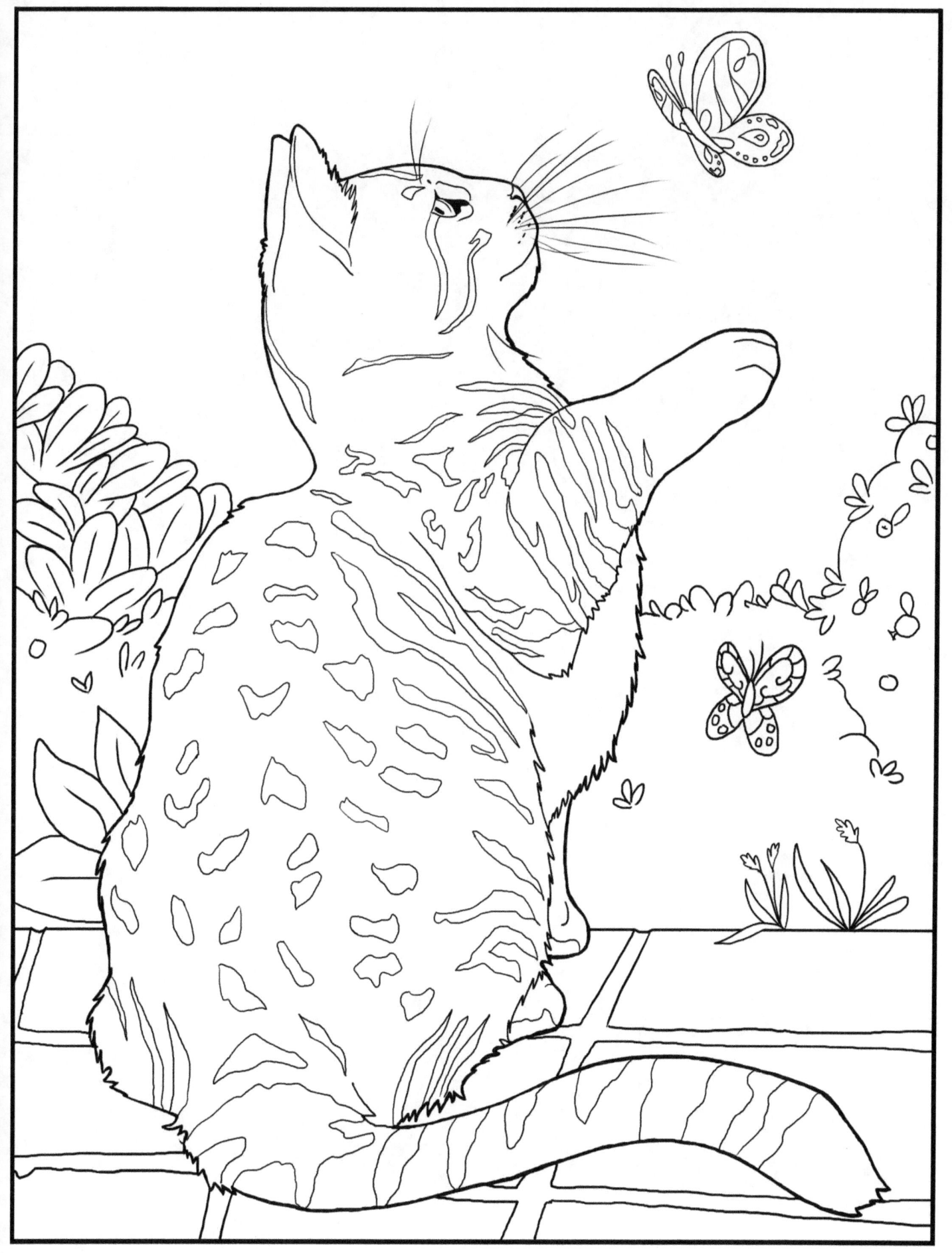

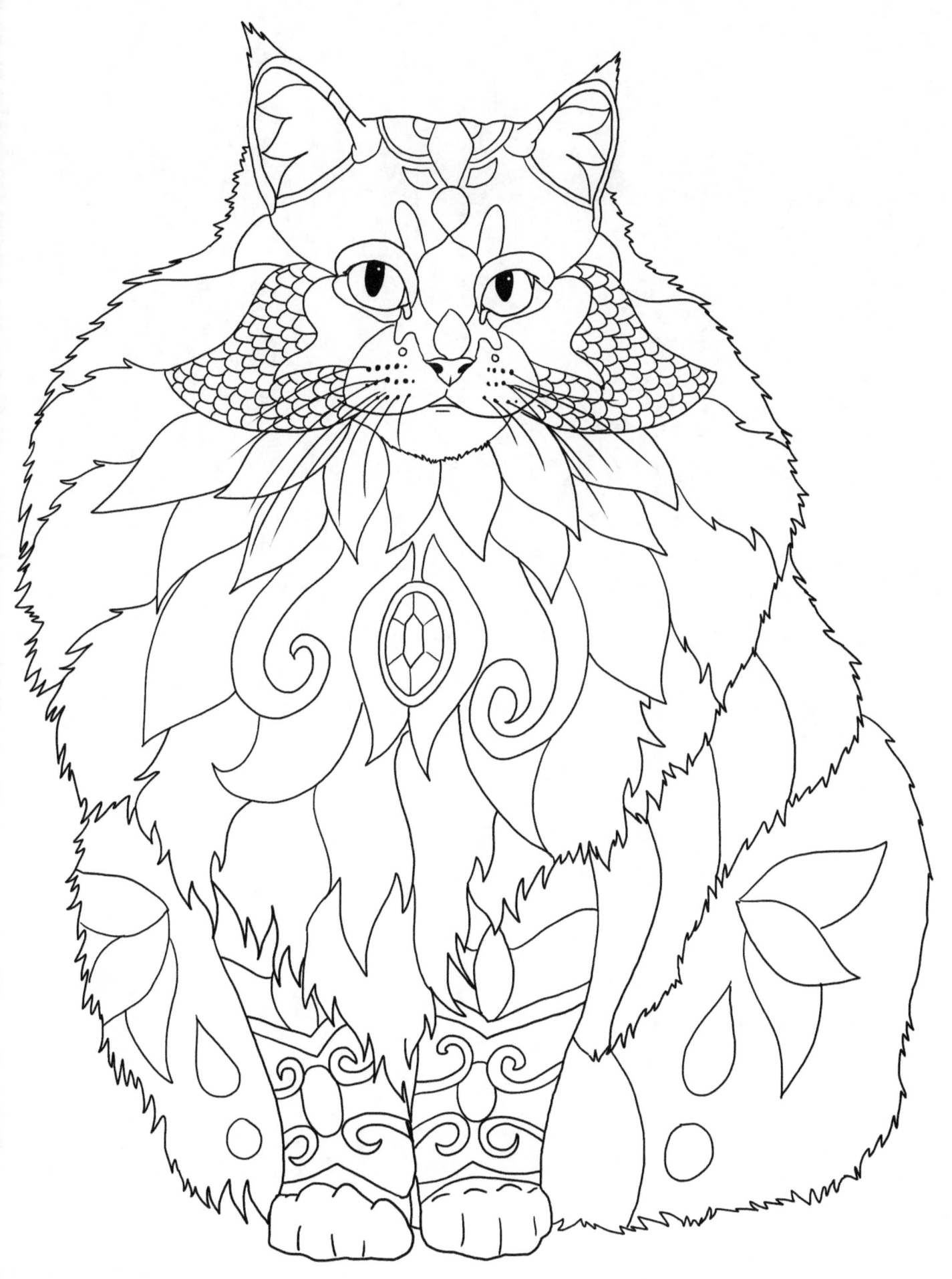

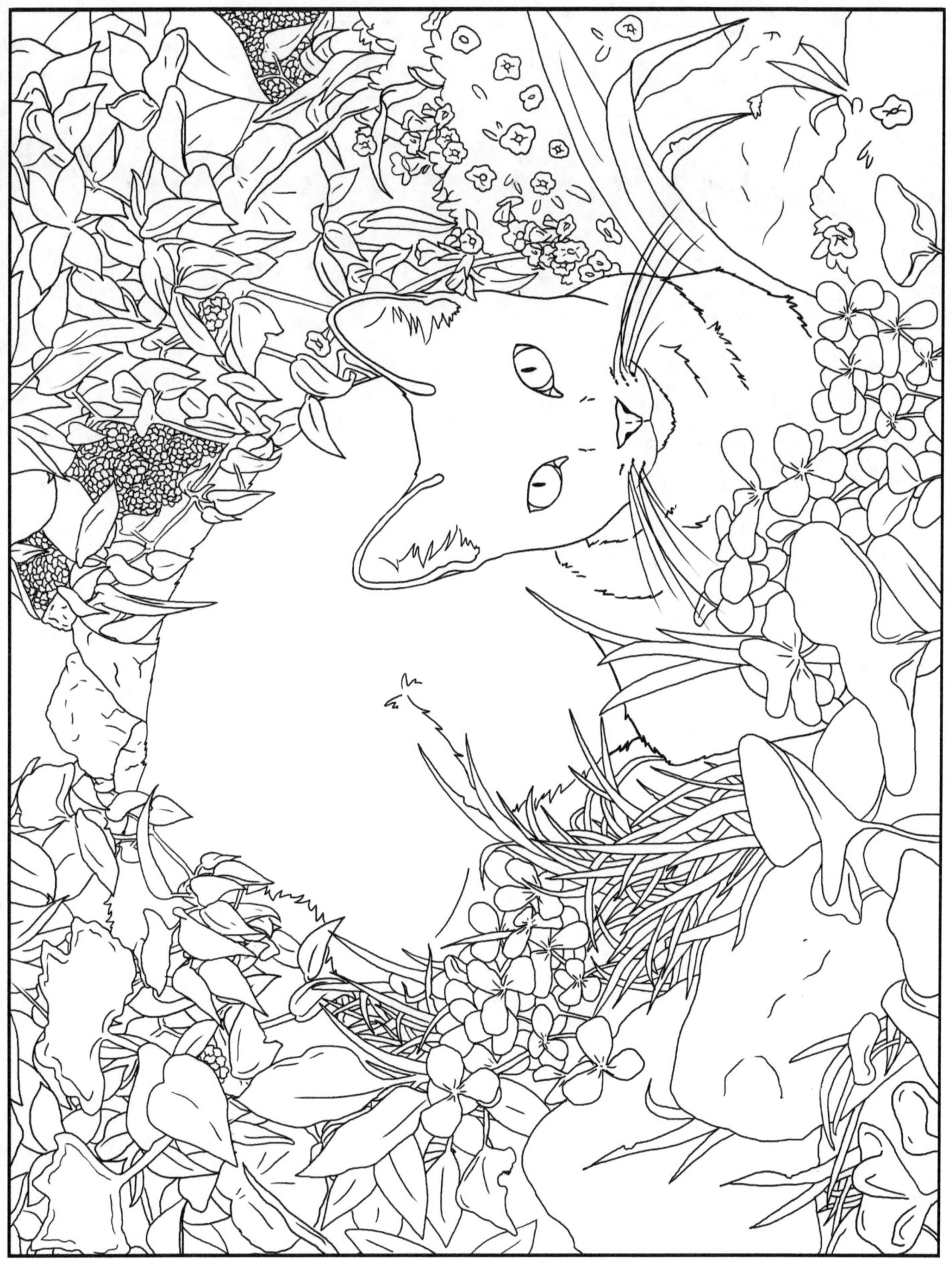

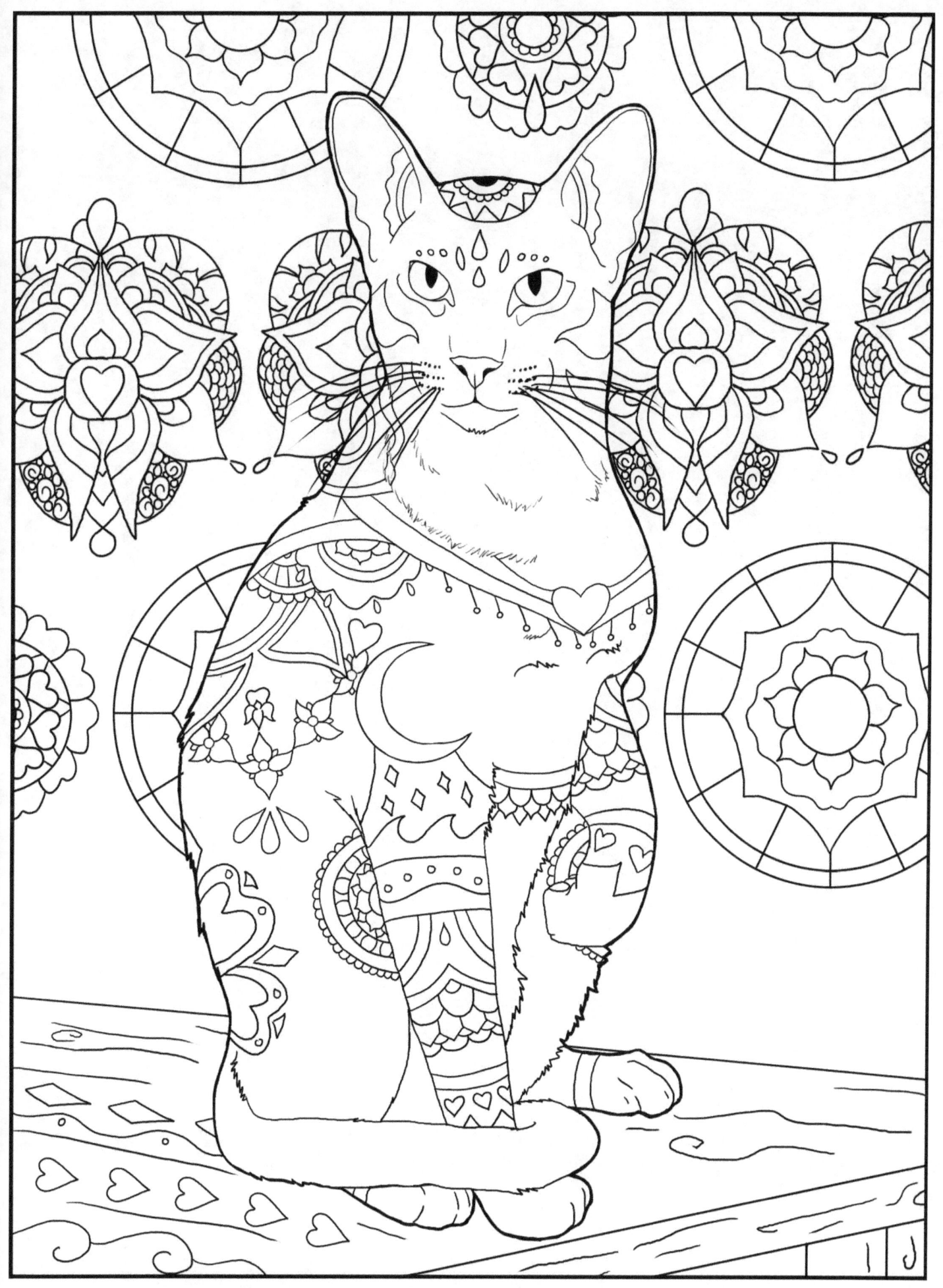

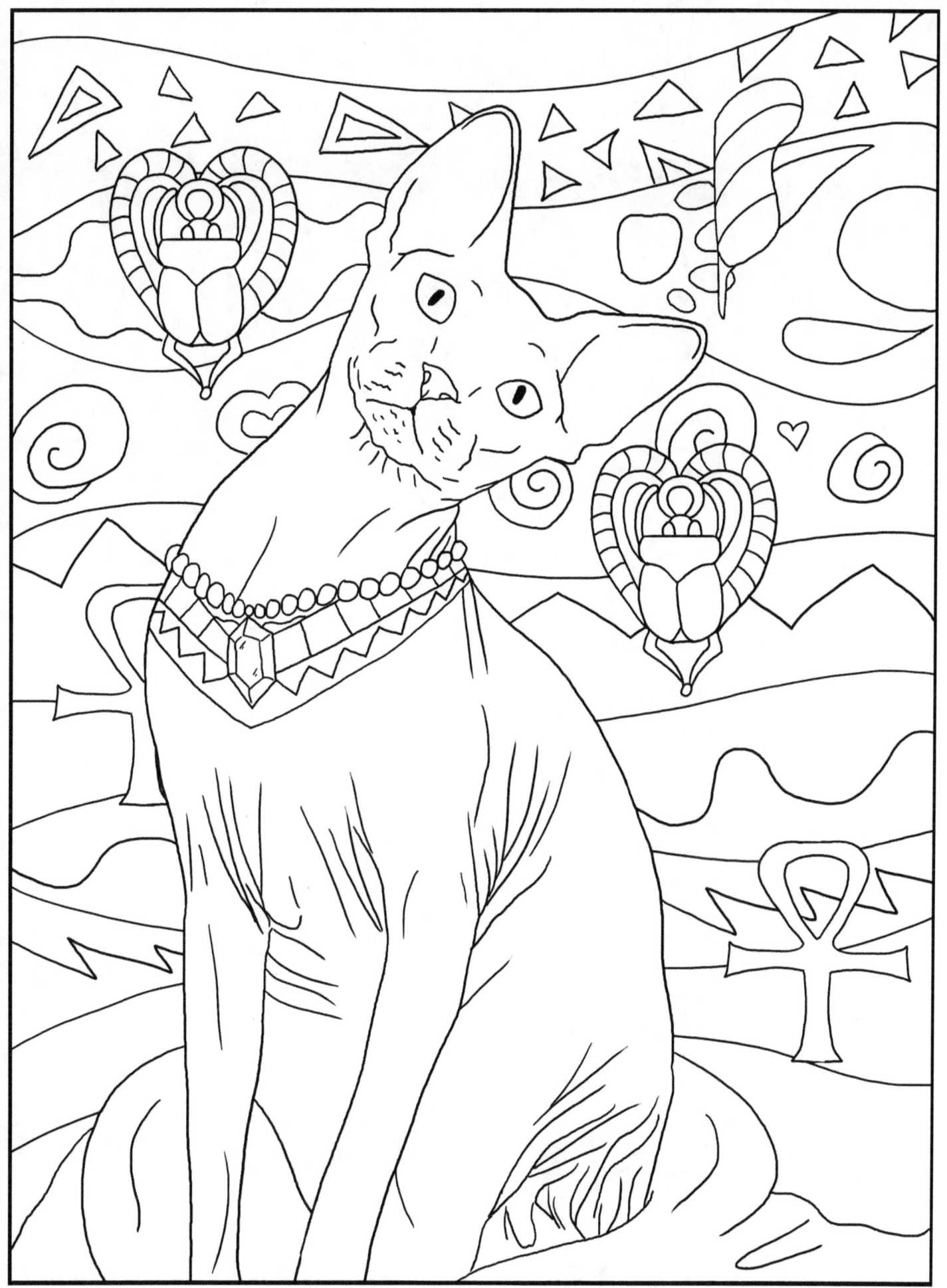

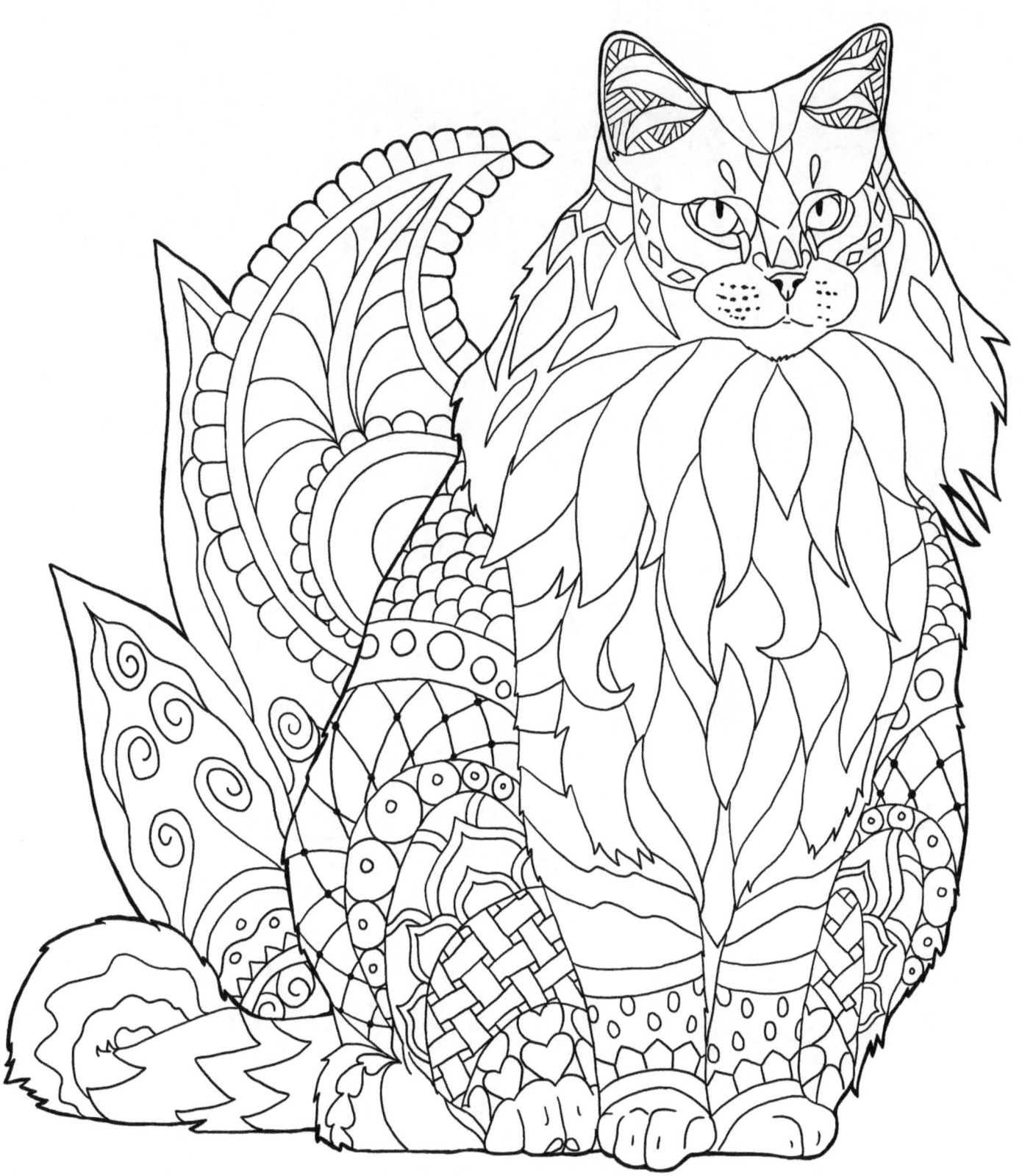

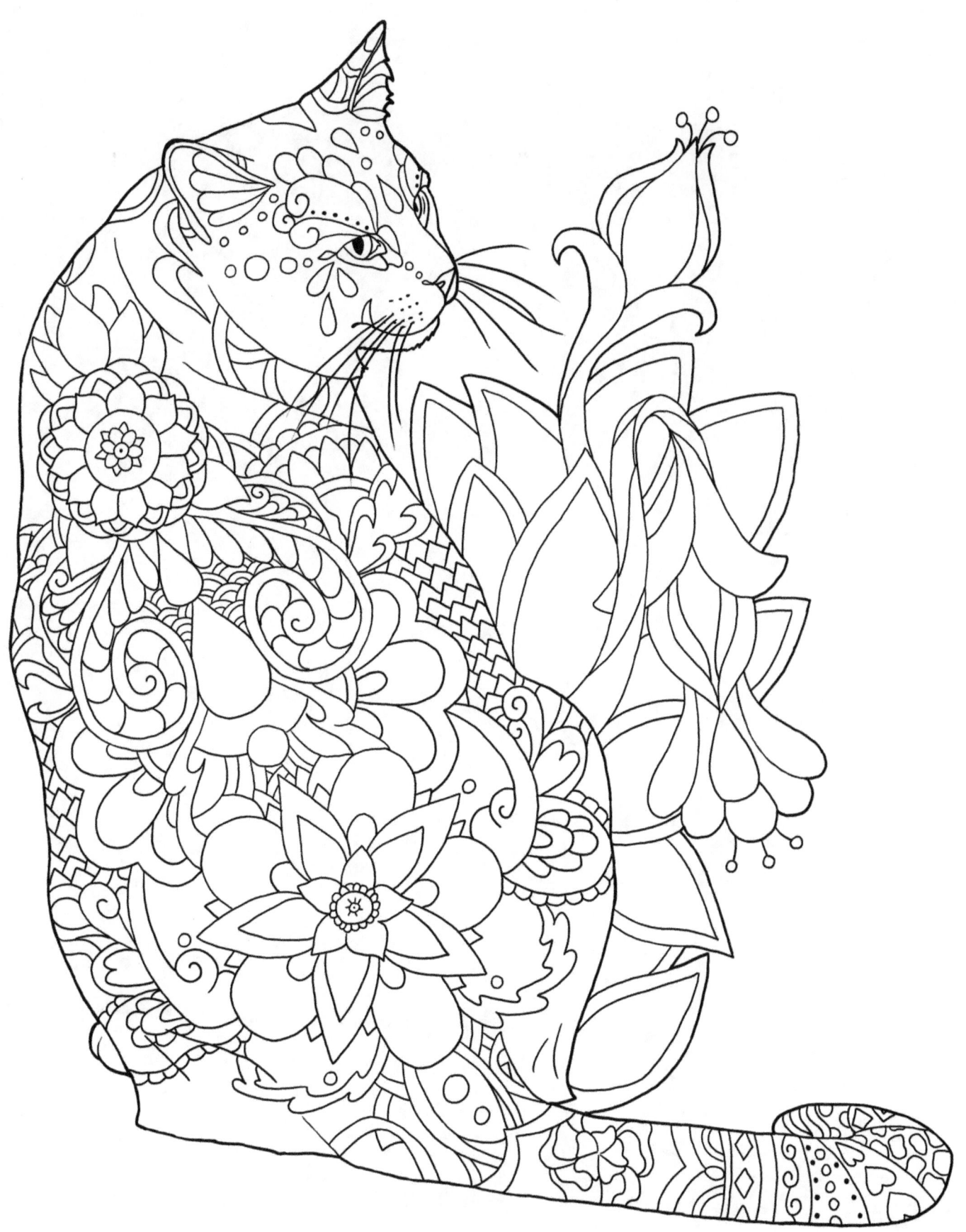

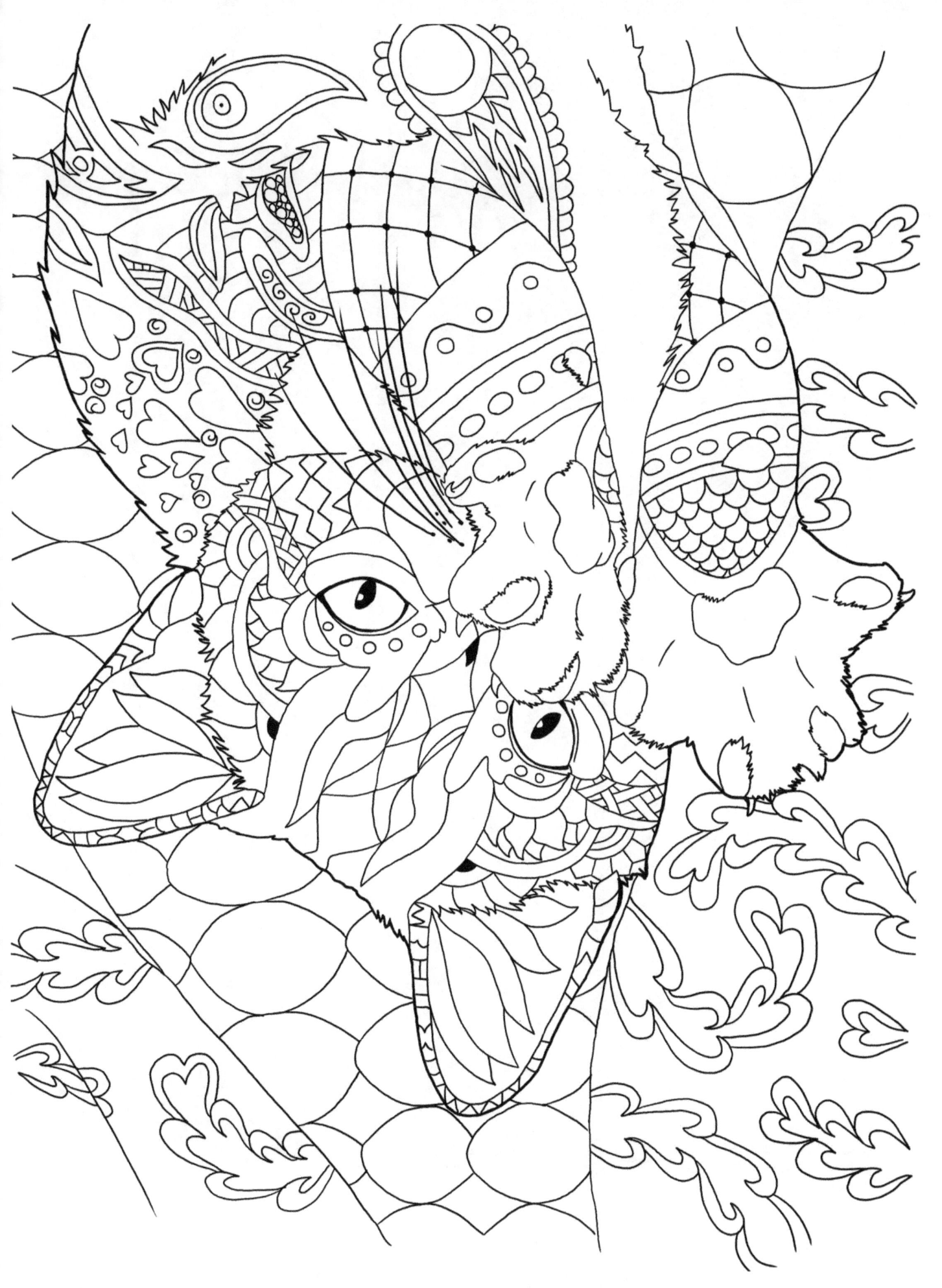

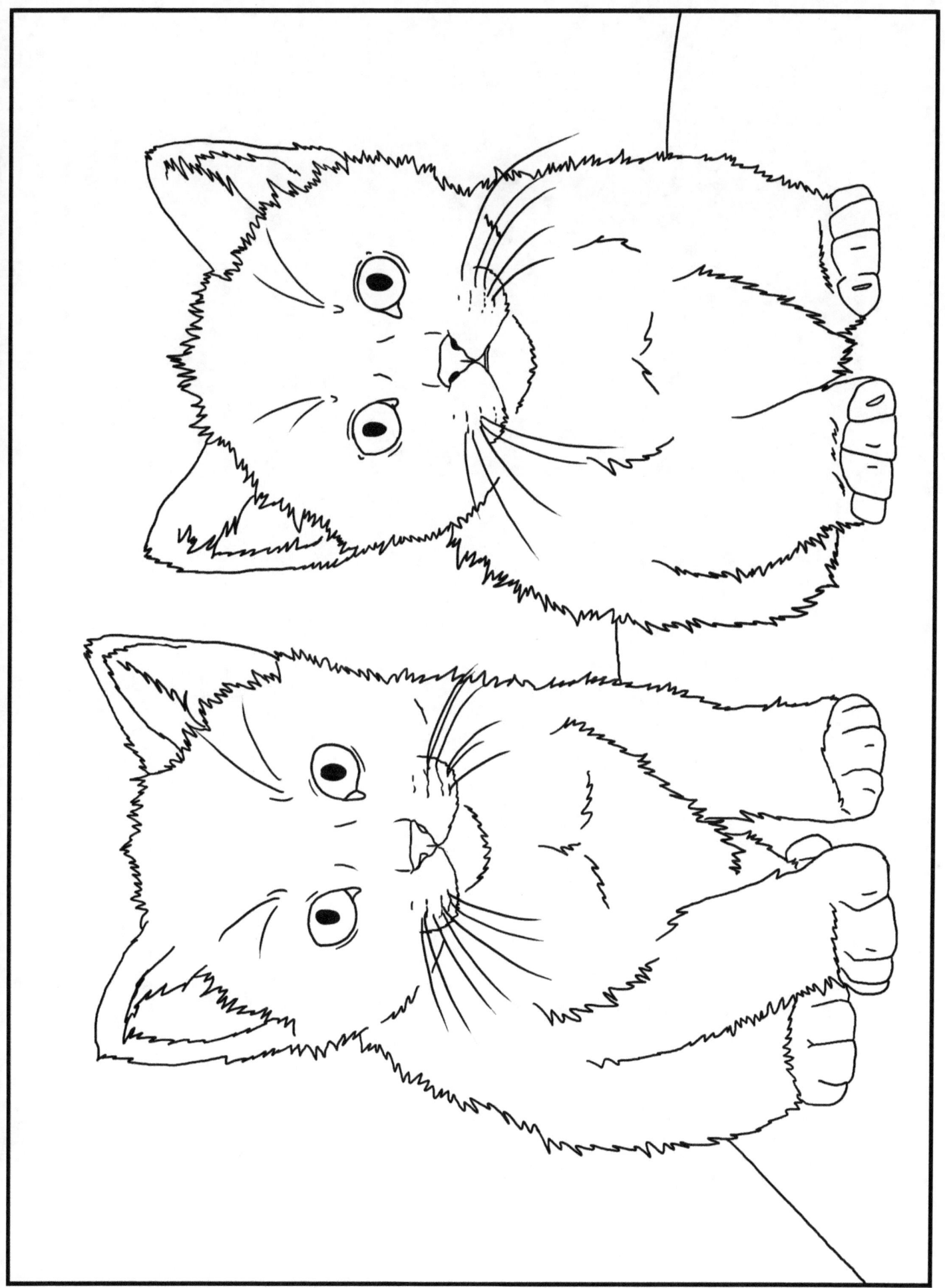

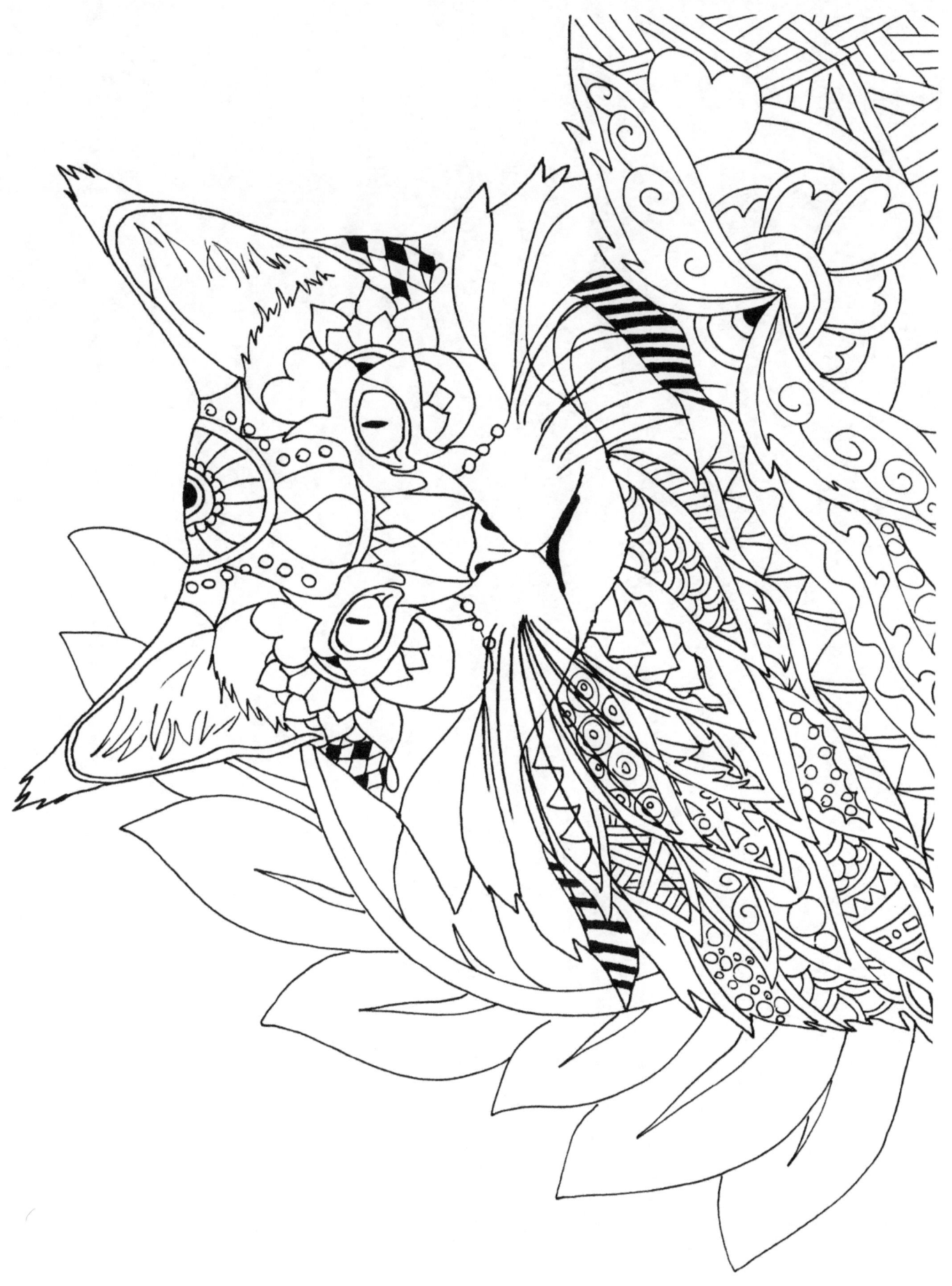

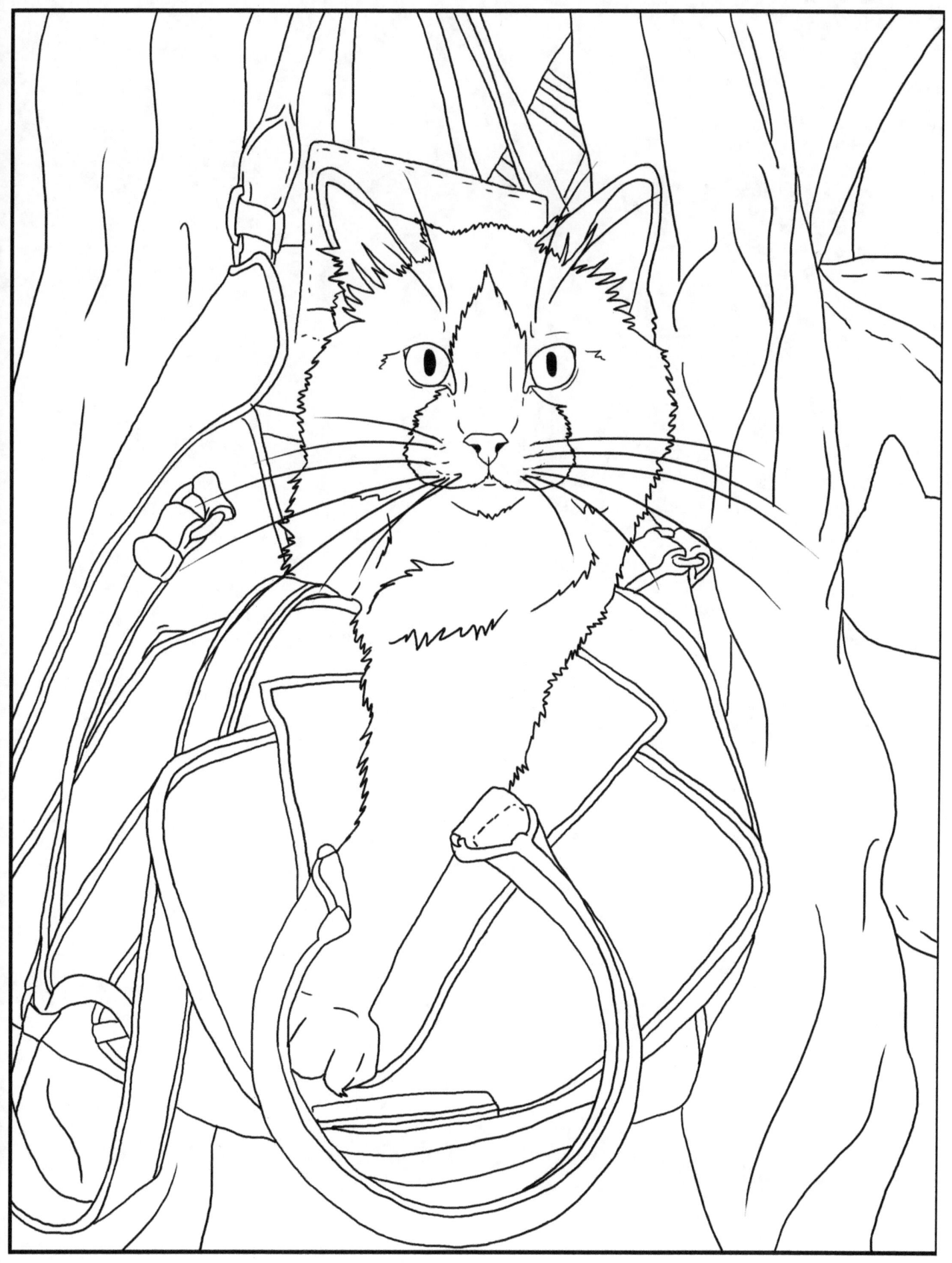

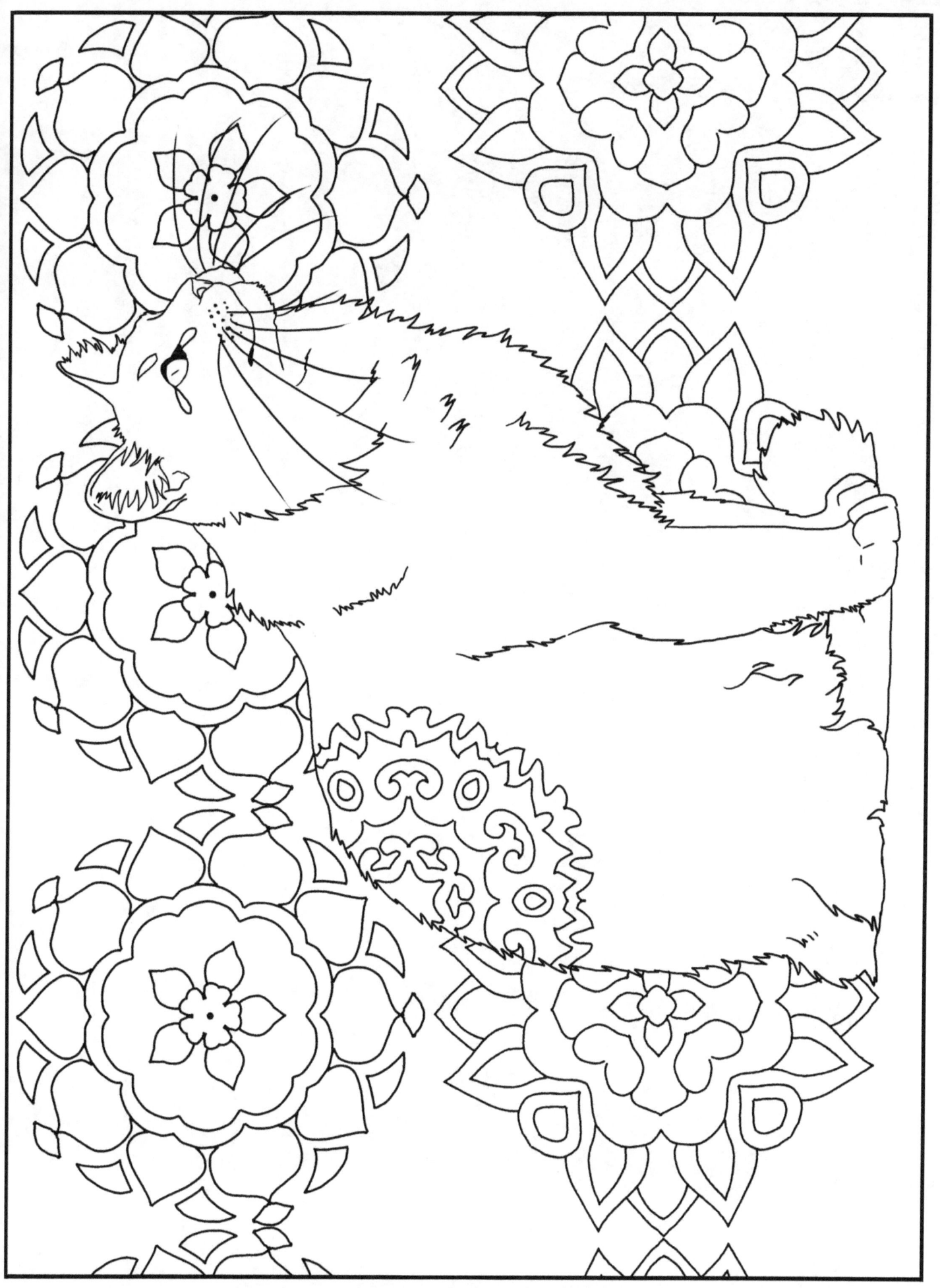

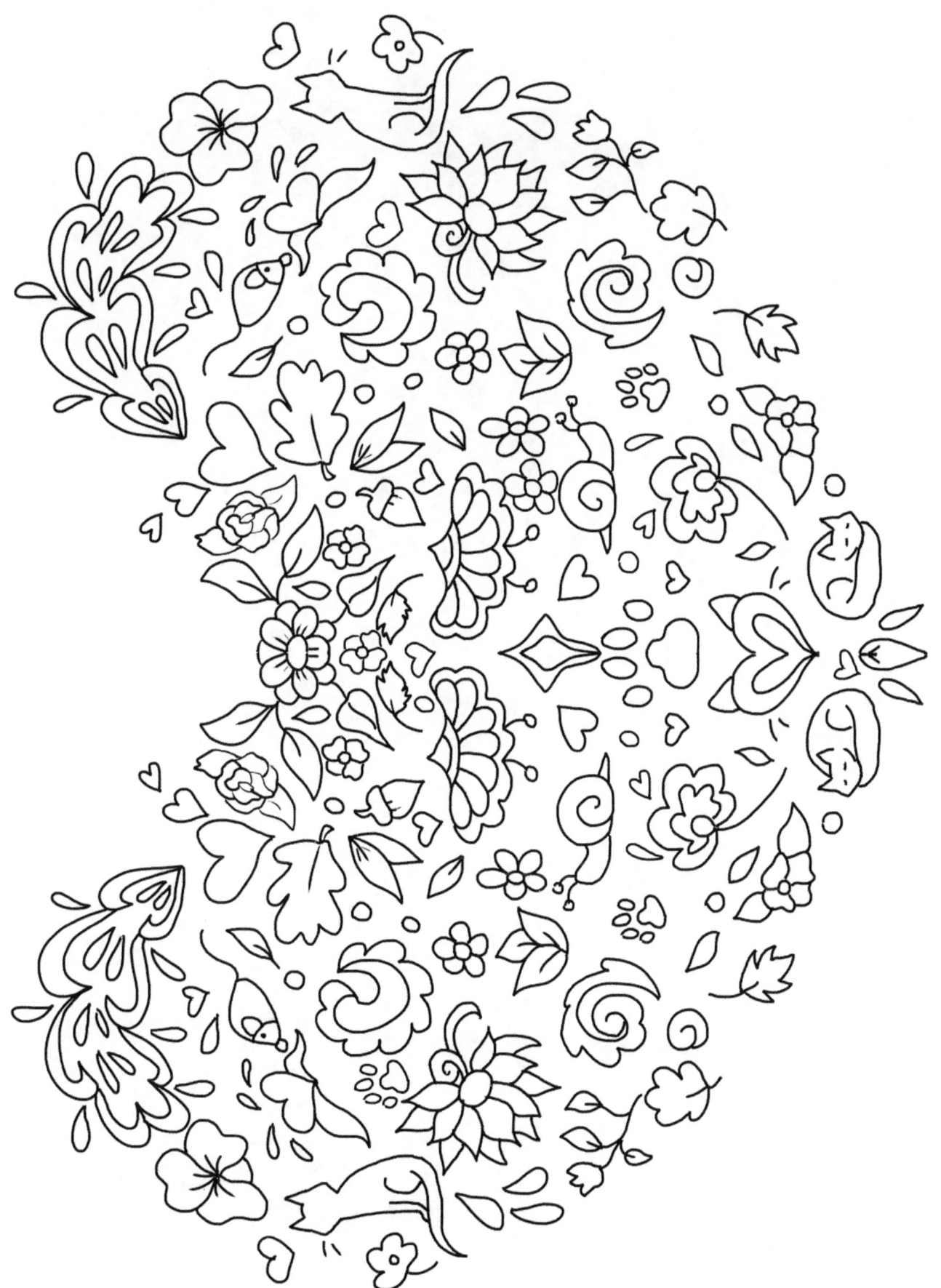

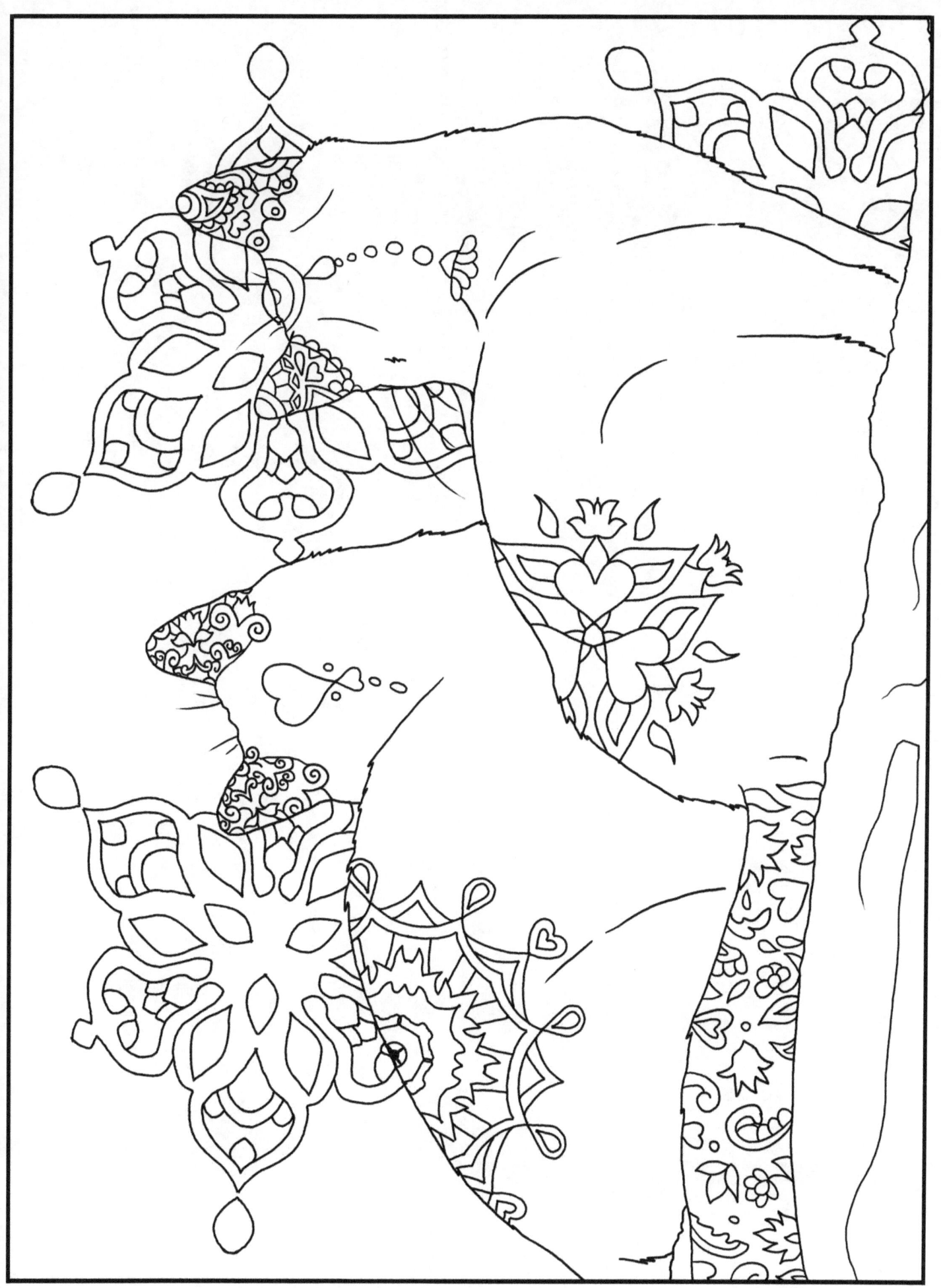

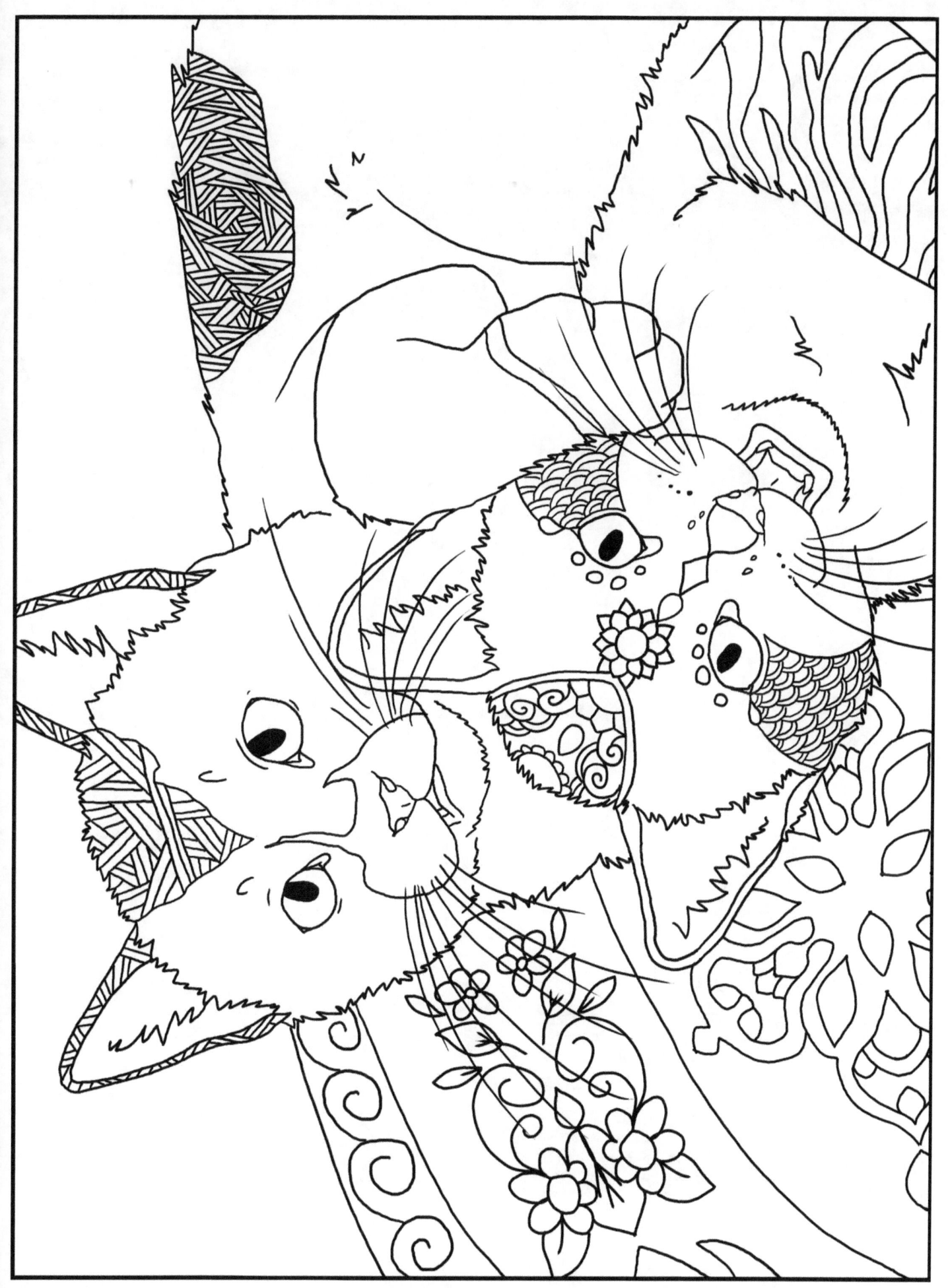

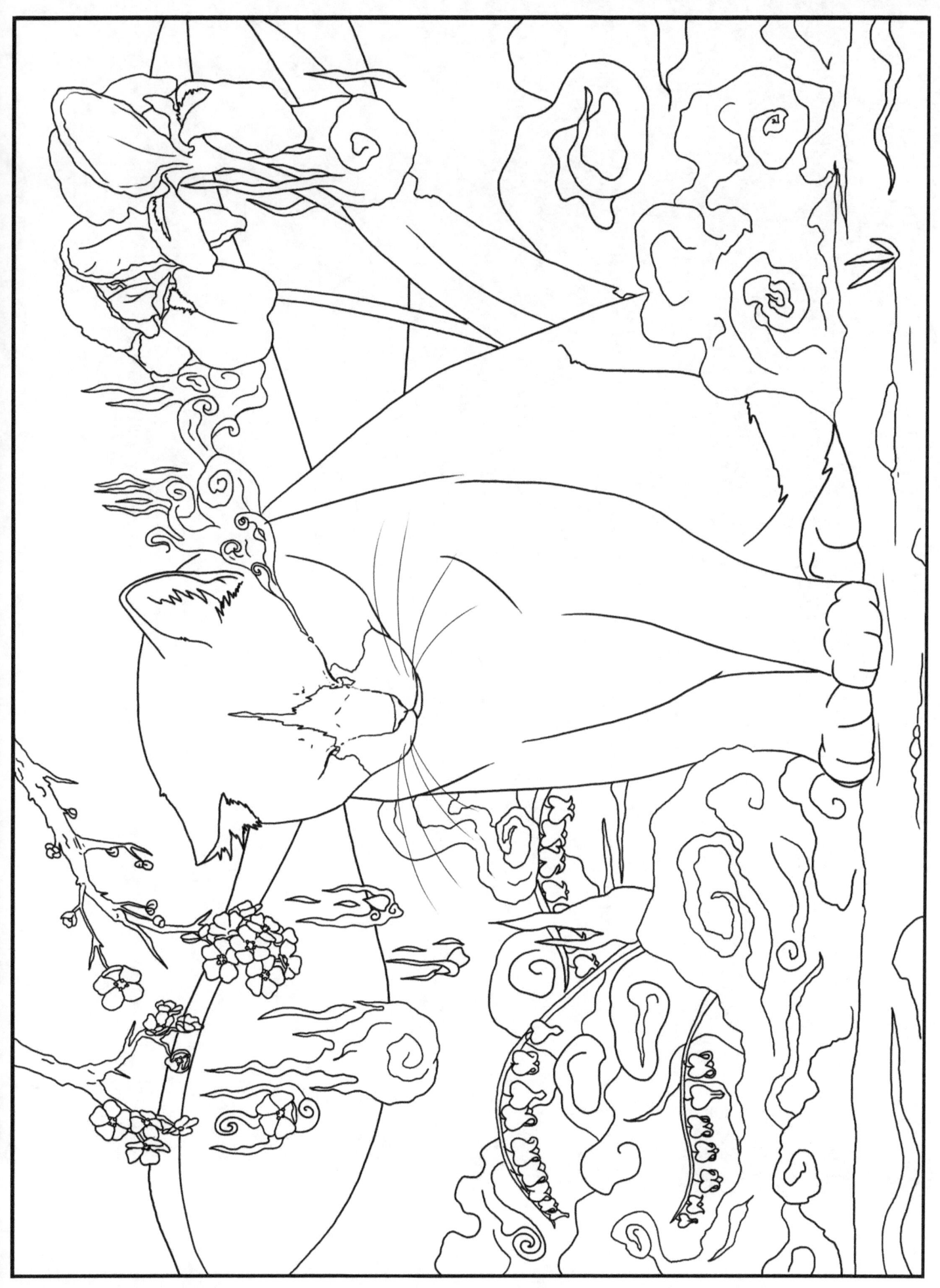

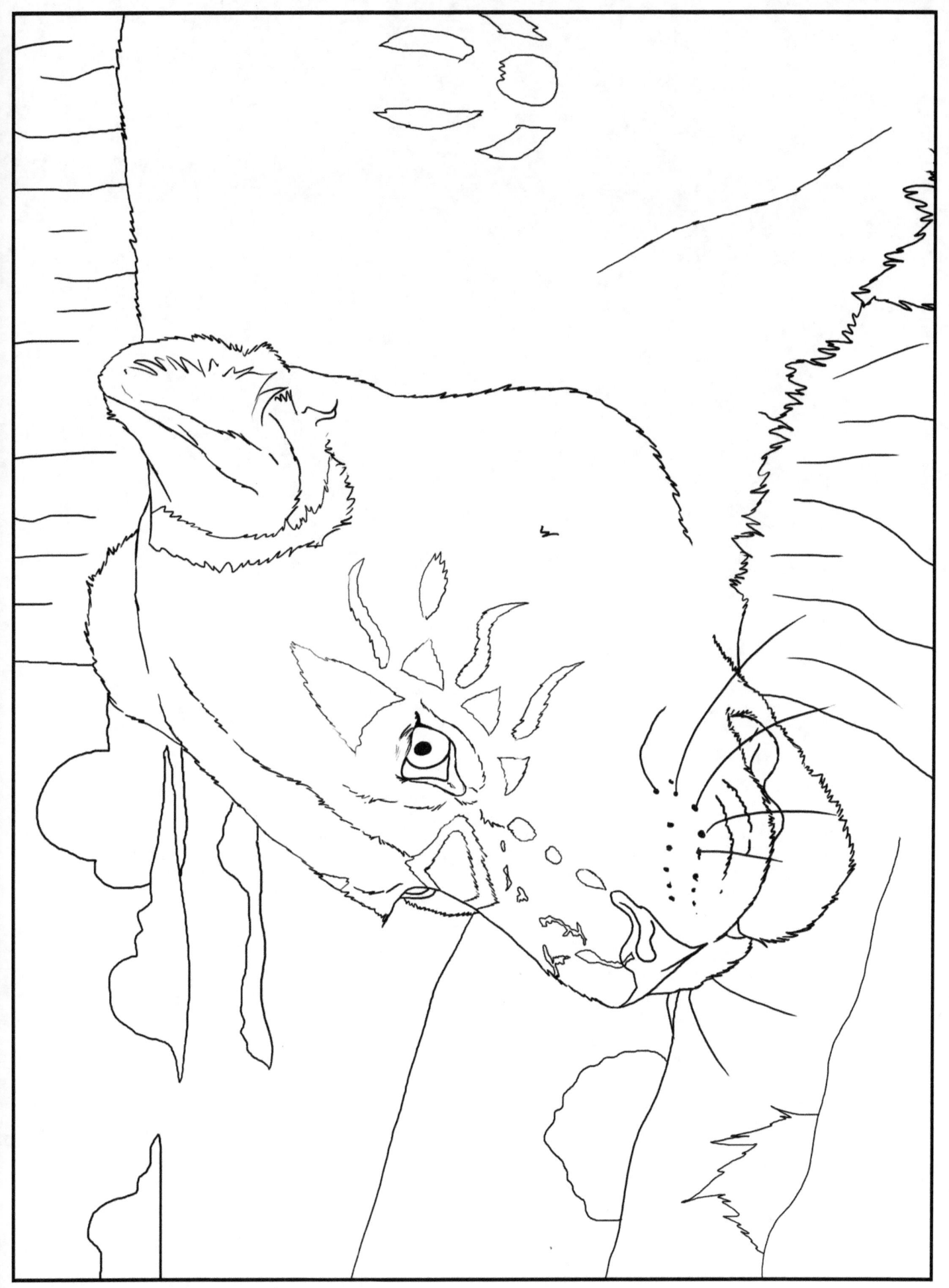

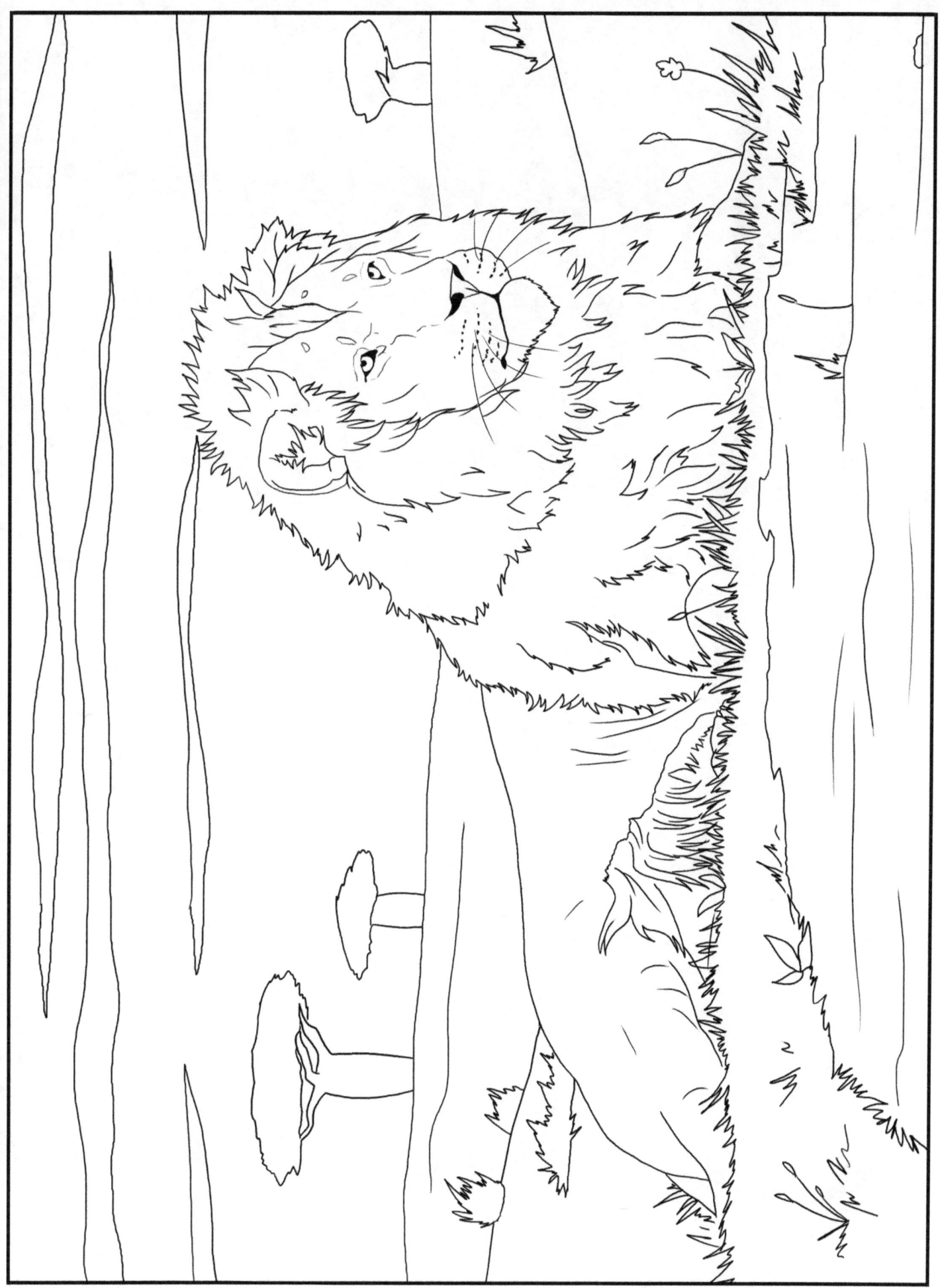

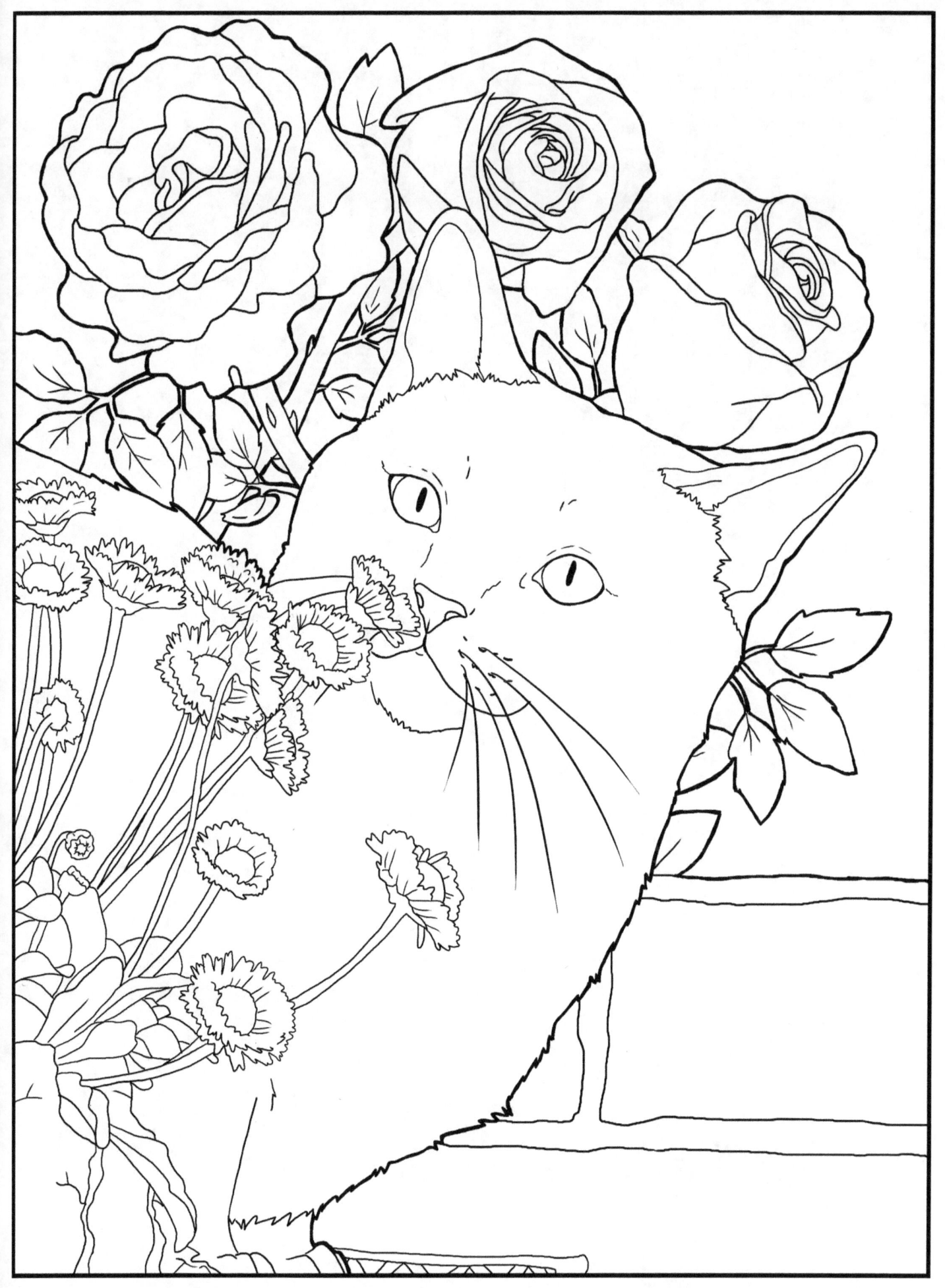

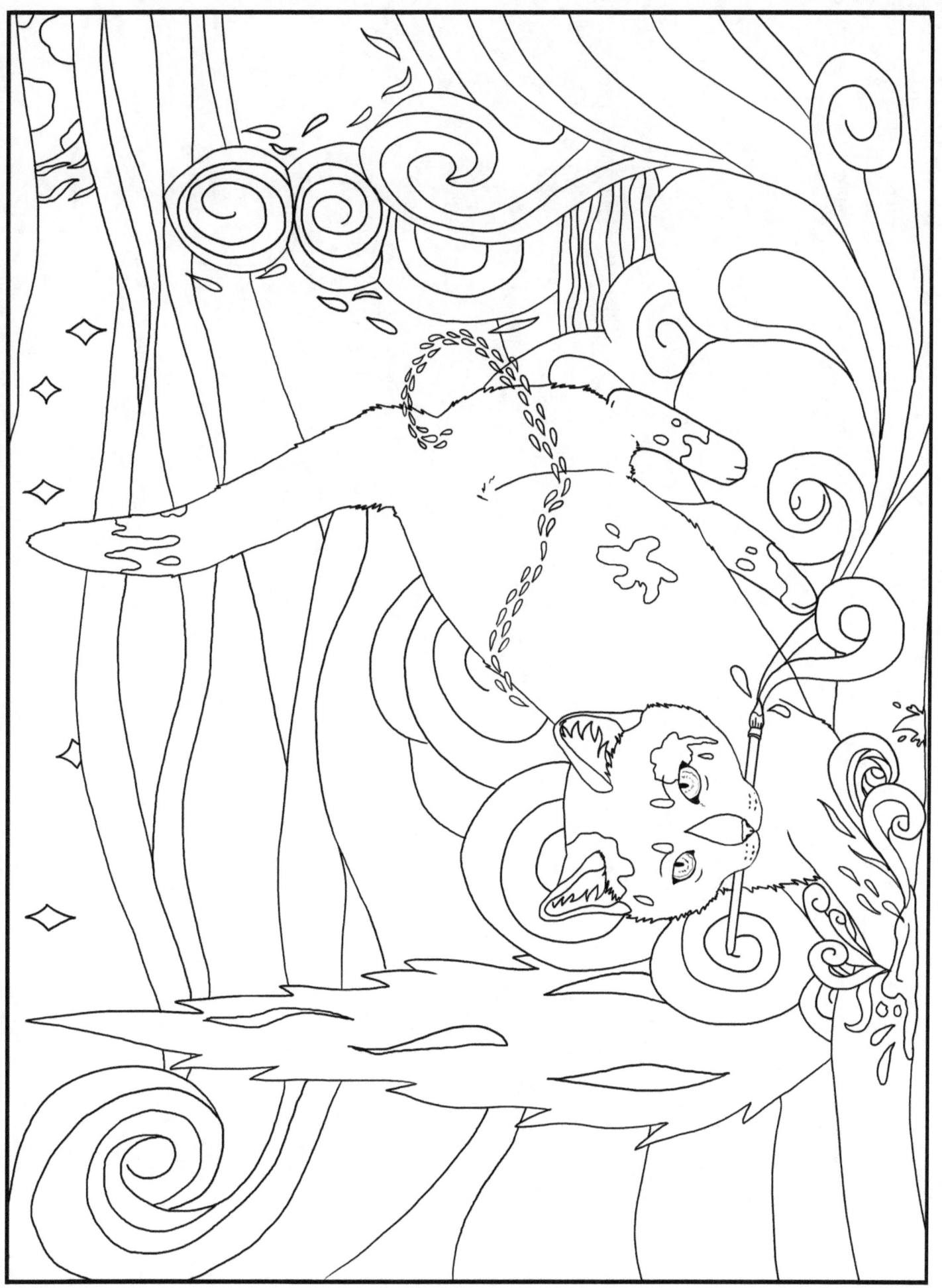

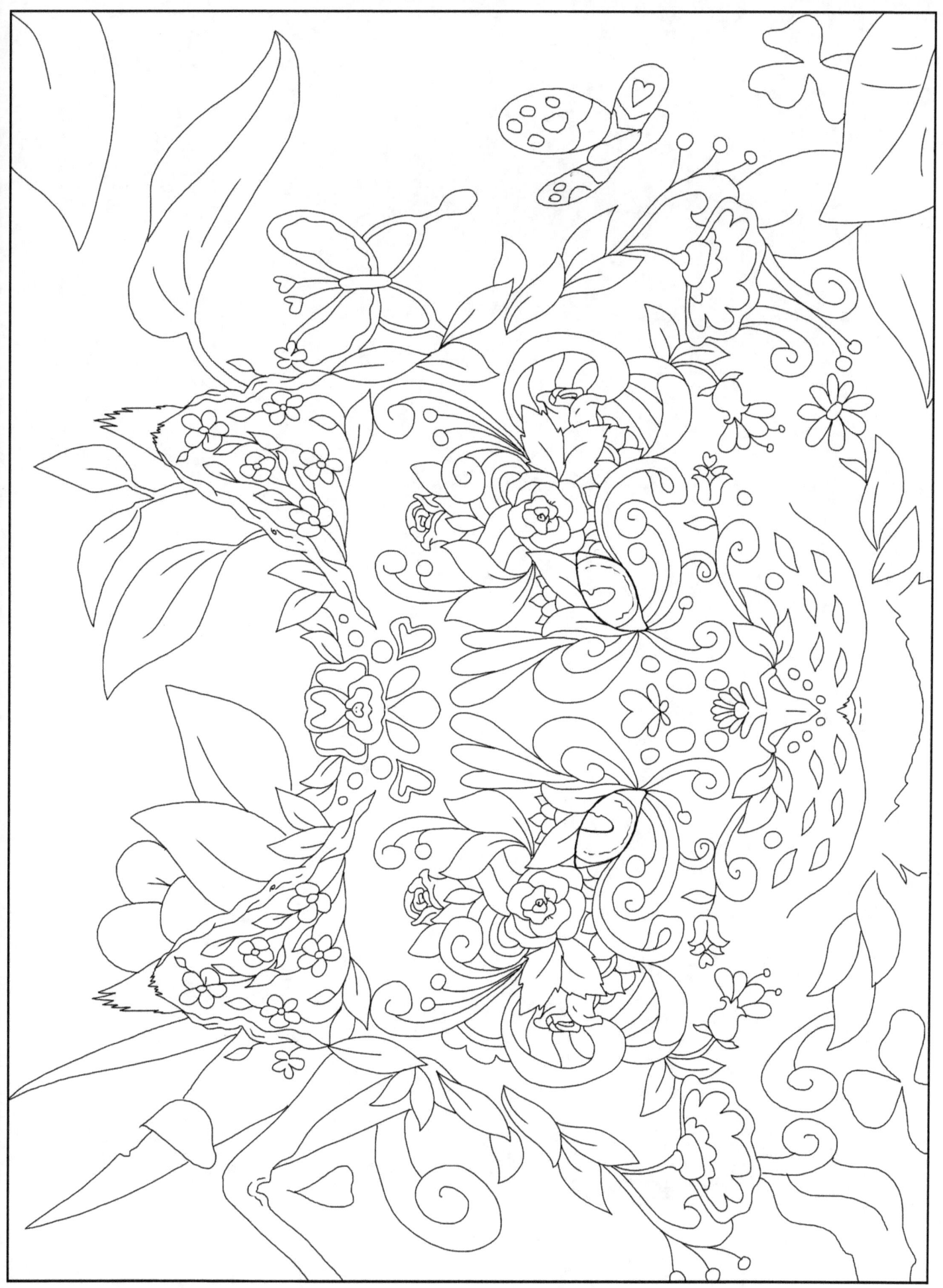

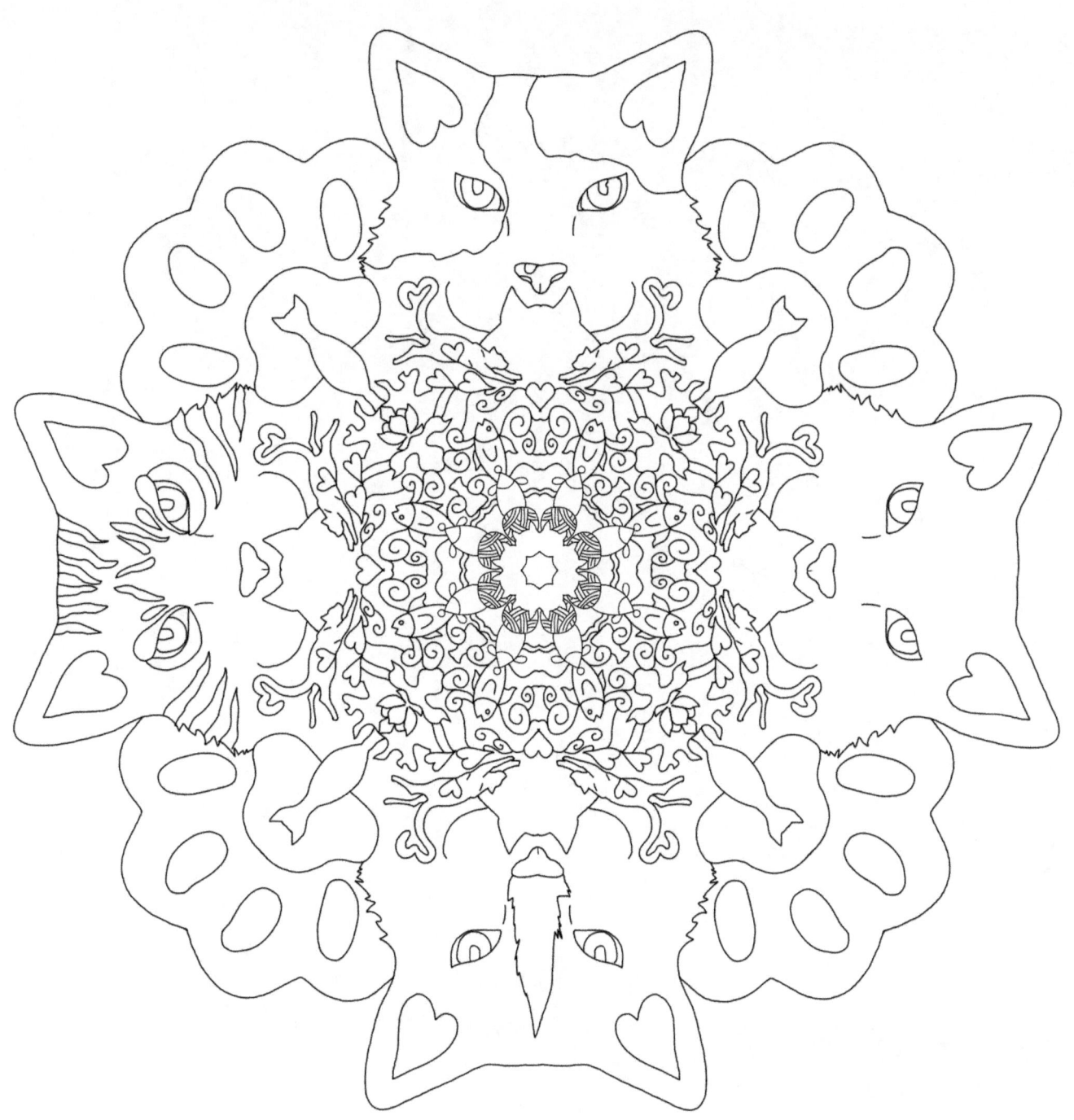

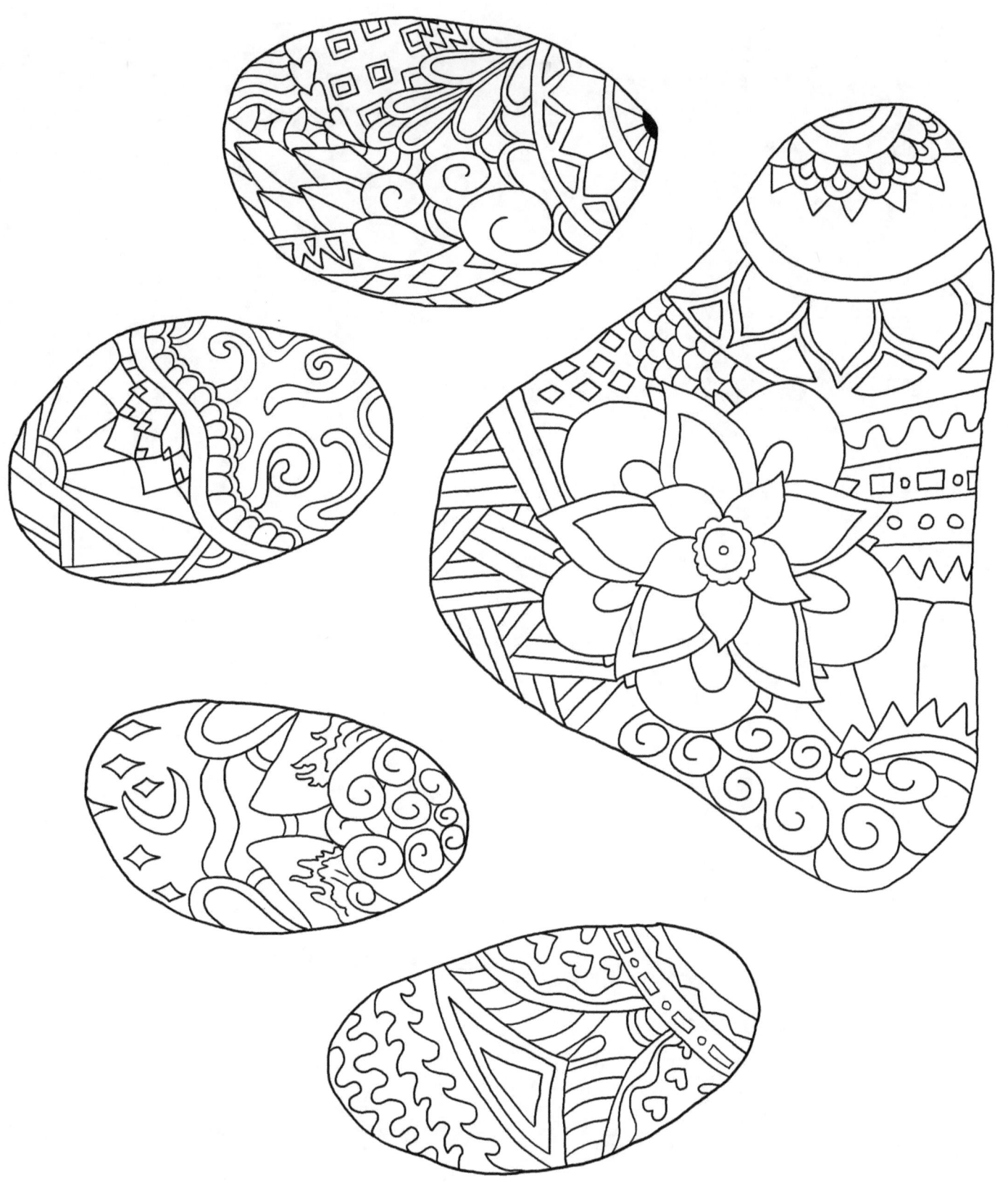

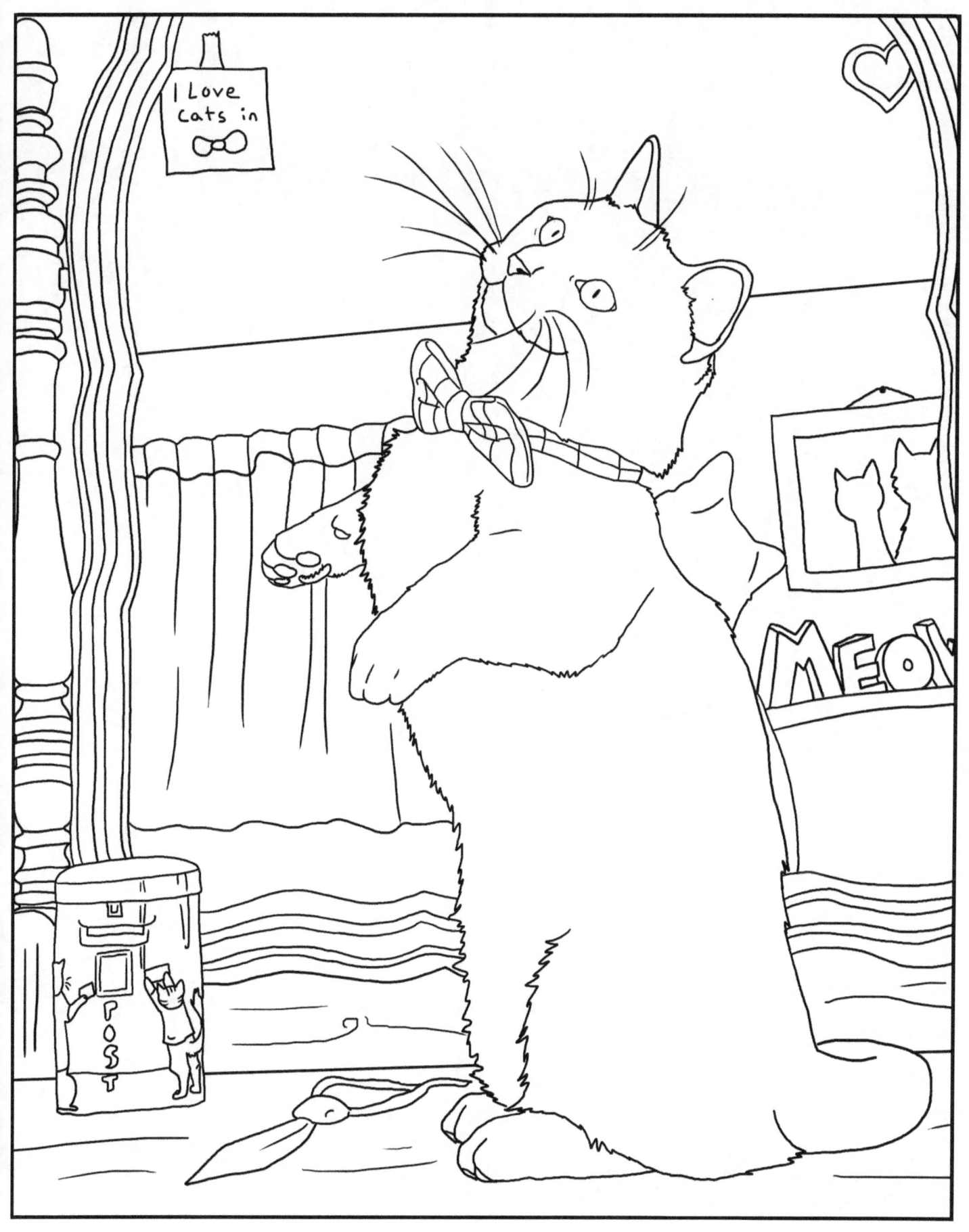

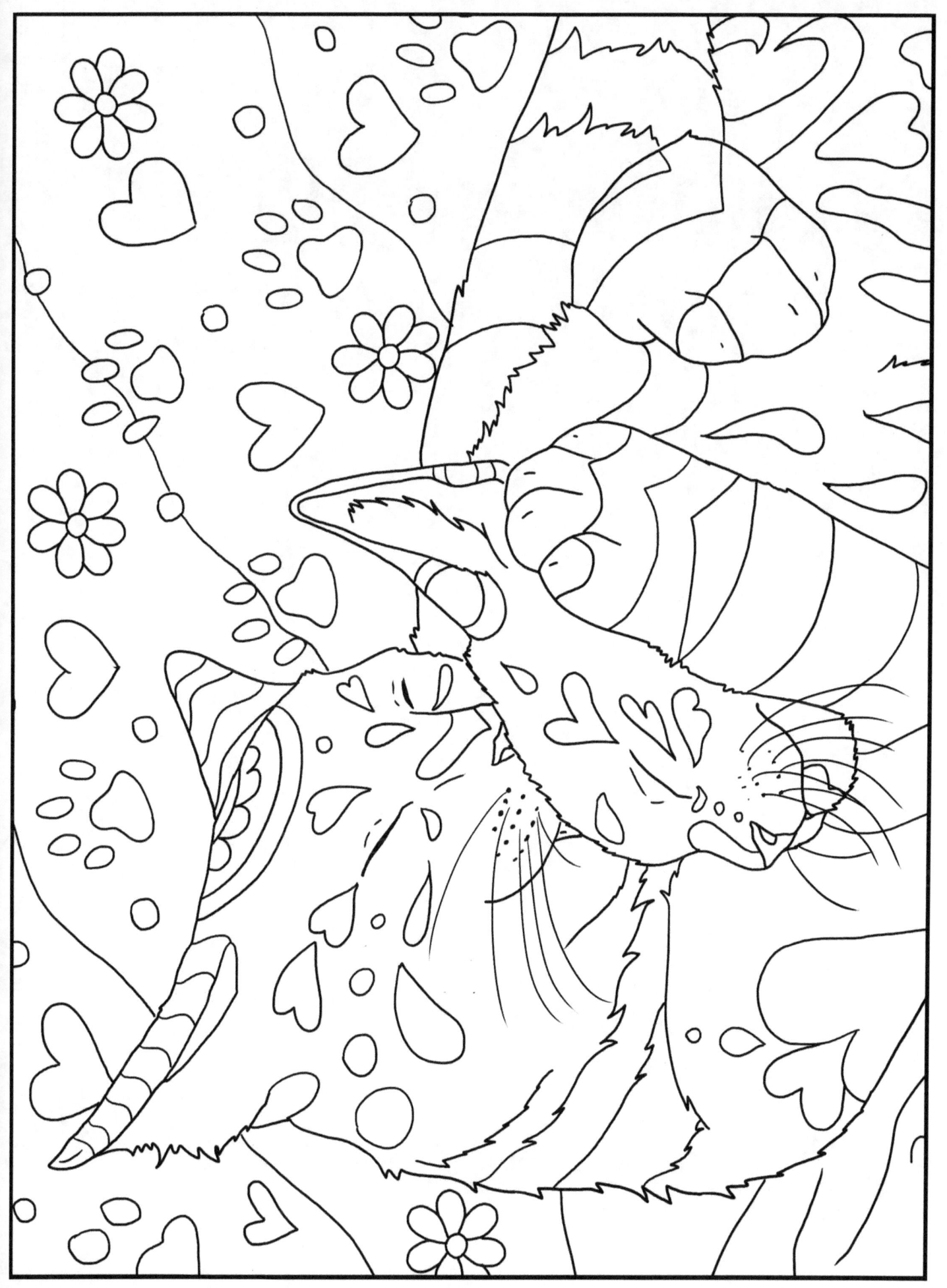

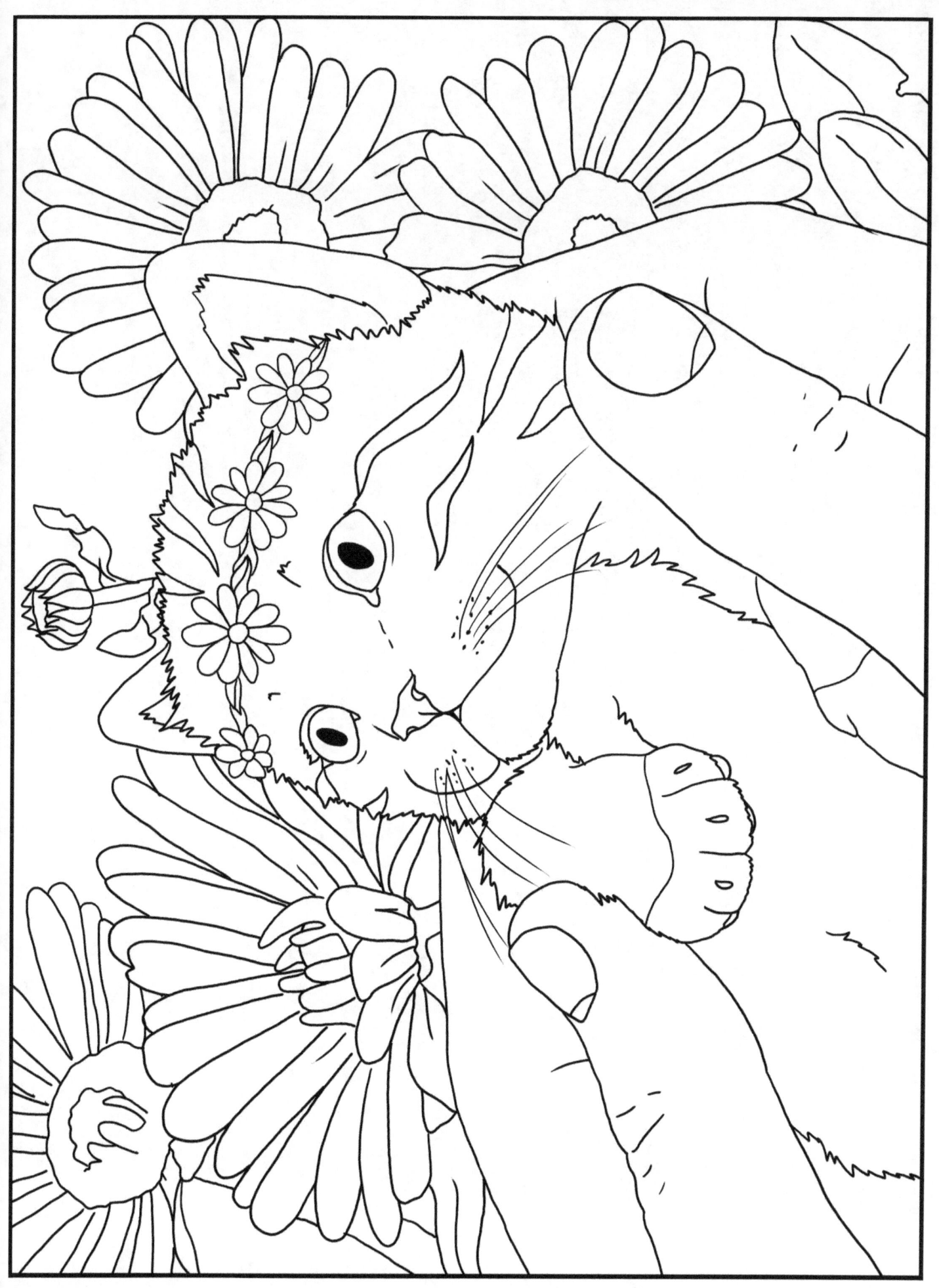

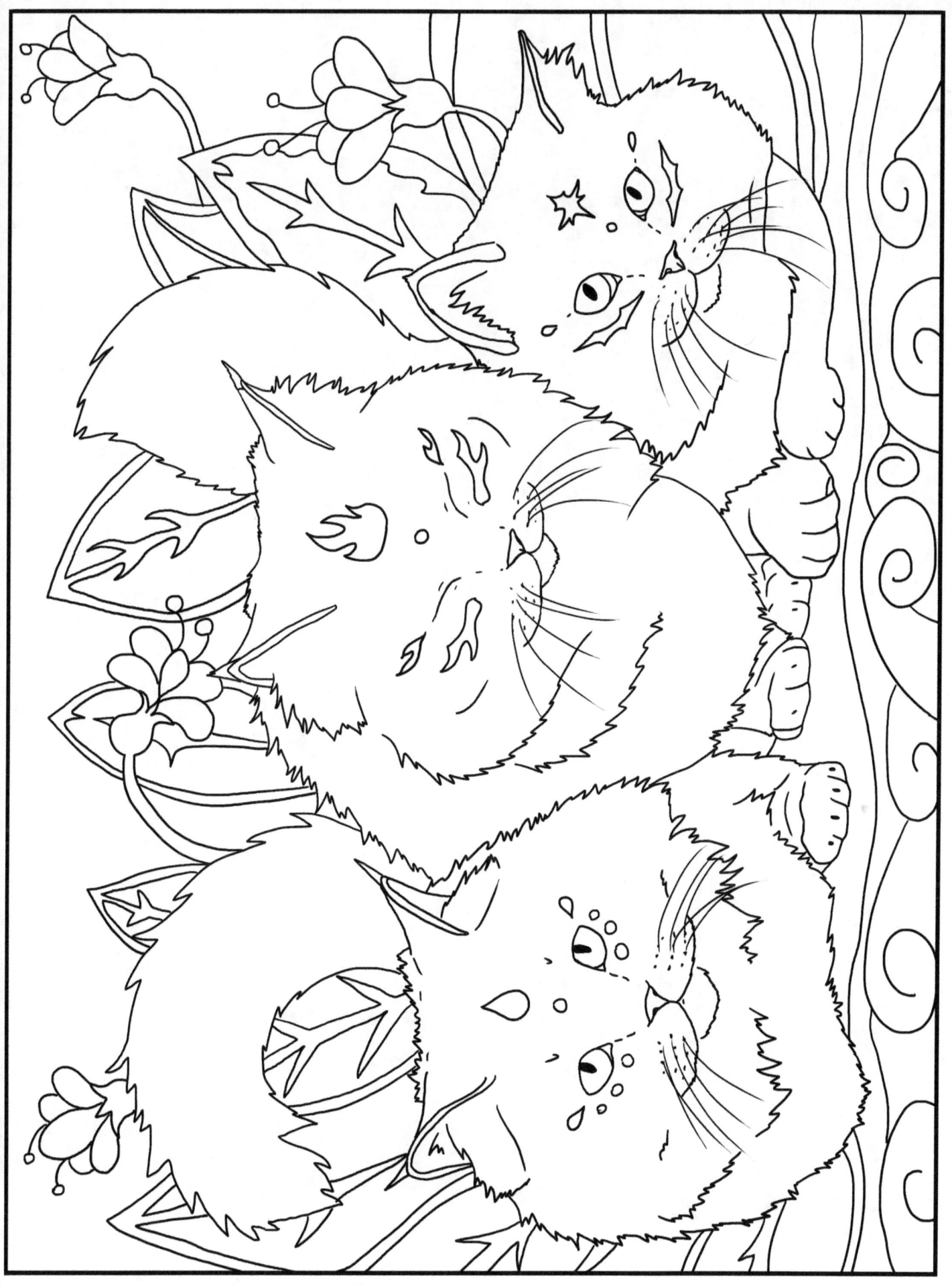

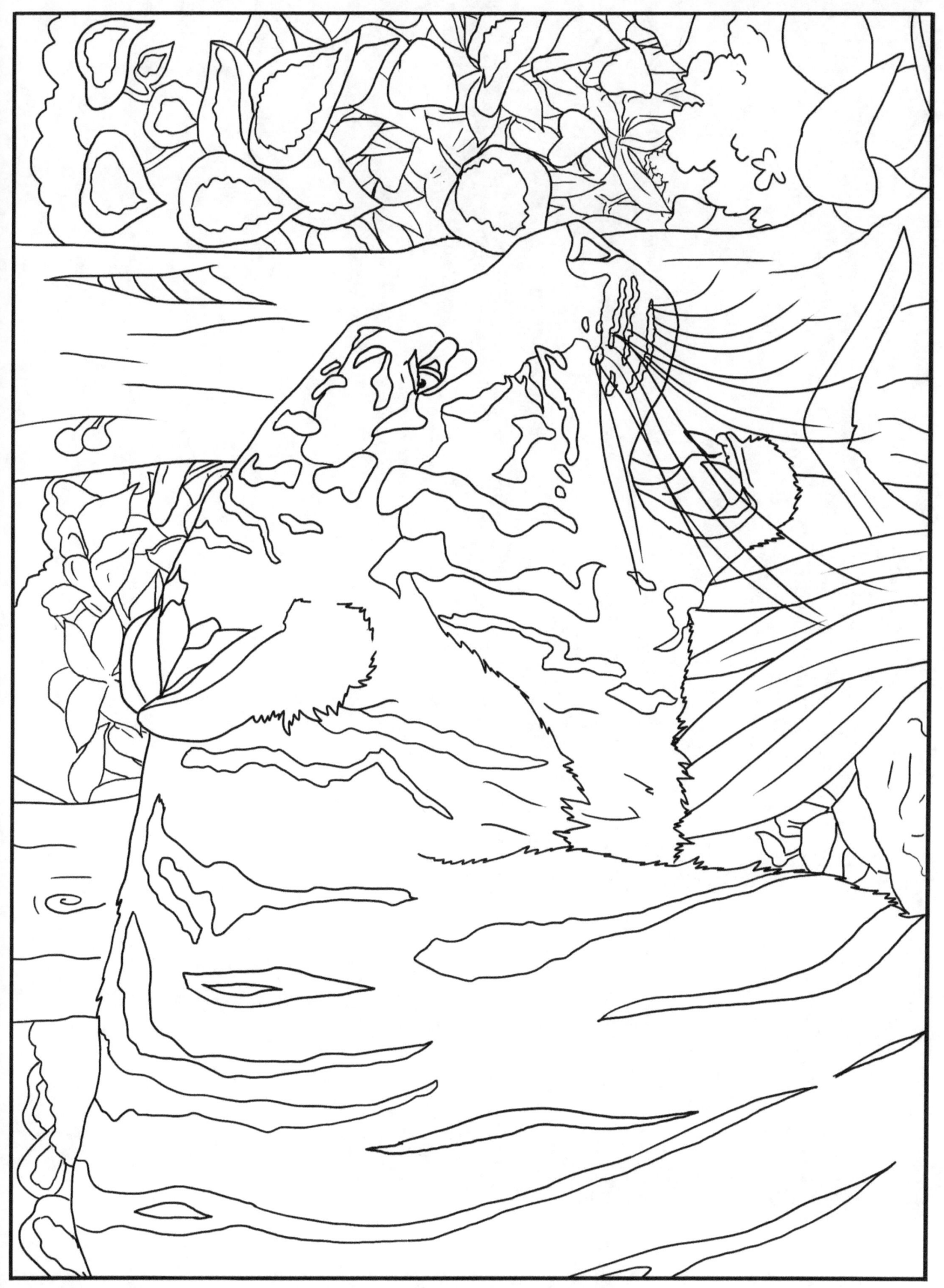

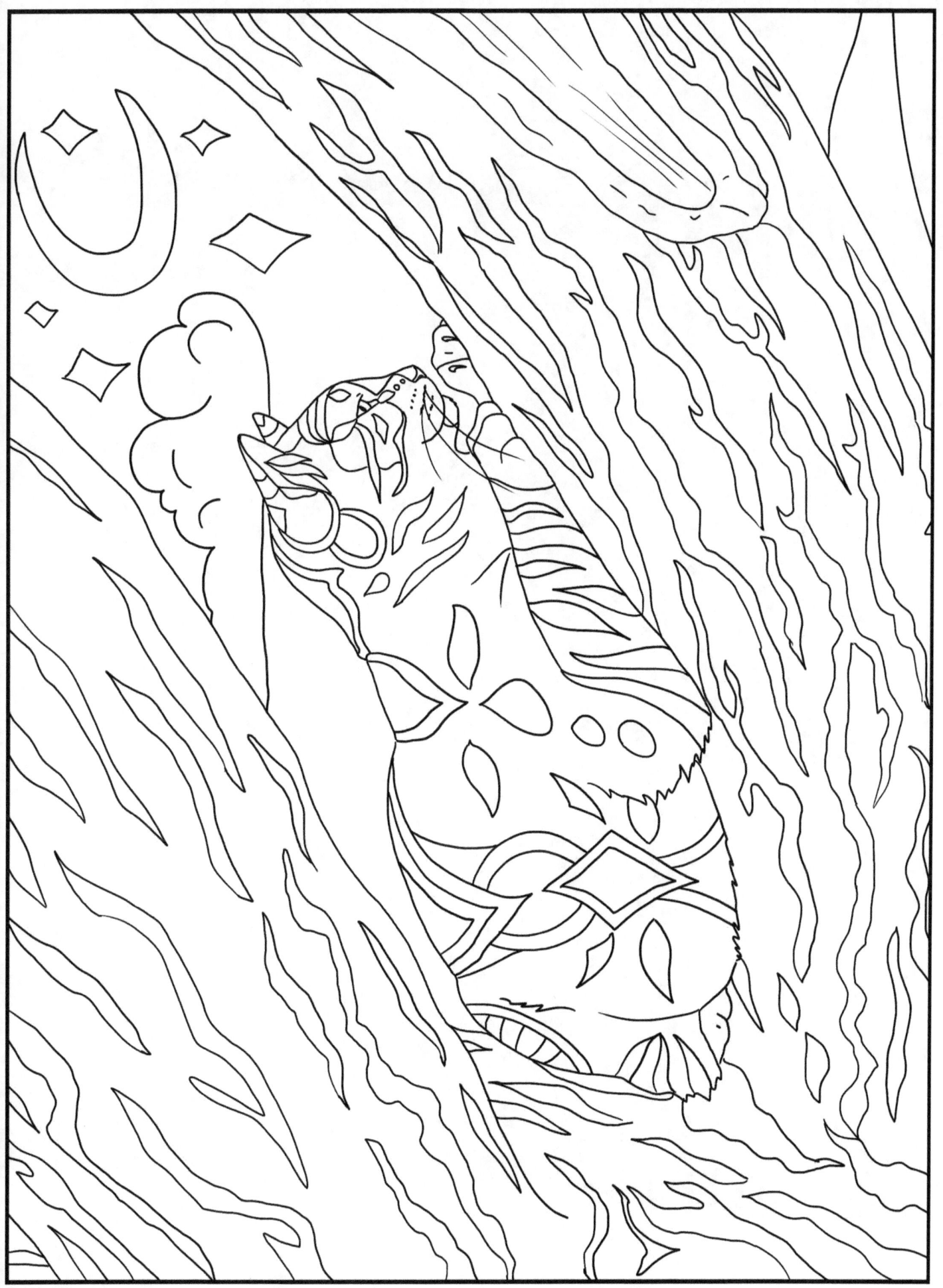

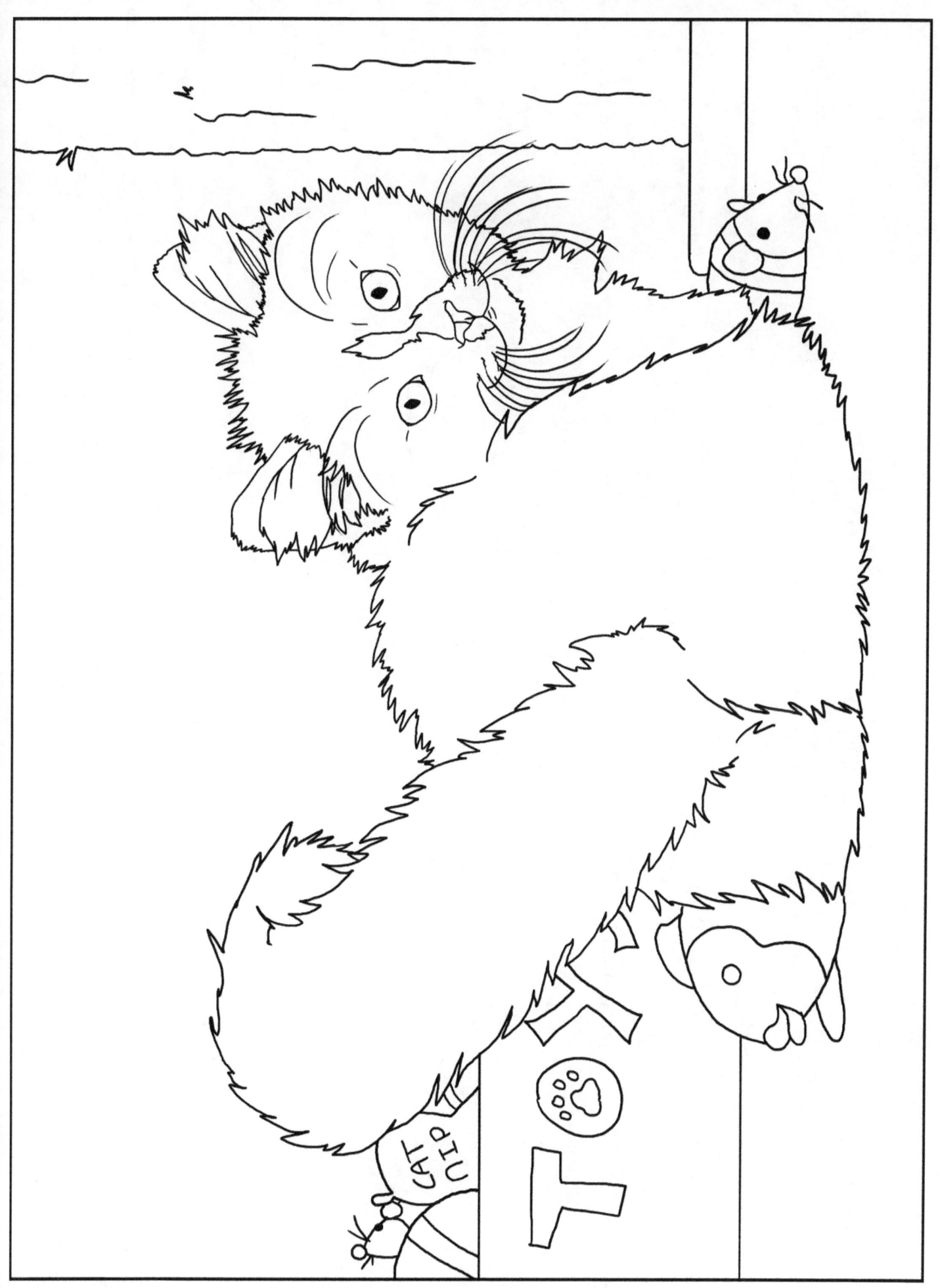

Credits

Special thanks to the lovely people who helped me create this book.
Photo reference credits listed by drawing order.
Not including the 'This Book Belongs To:' page.
All other drawings from personal references.

Drawing 2. "Brandy" Jim Peters fashionphotographyonline.com
Pittsburgh, PA

Drawing 3. "Boonie" Sara Mertens

Drawing 4. "Trevor" Melanie Jordan

Drawing 5. "Turtle" Kristina Saucedo

Drawing 10. "Santana" Sam McConnell

Drawing 11. "Liam" Cathy Porter

Drawing 27. "Shortie, Midget and Minnie" Darlene Lewis

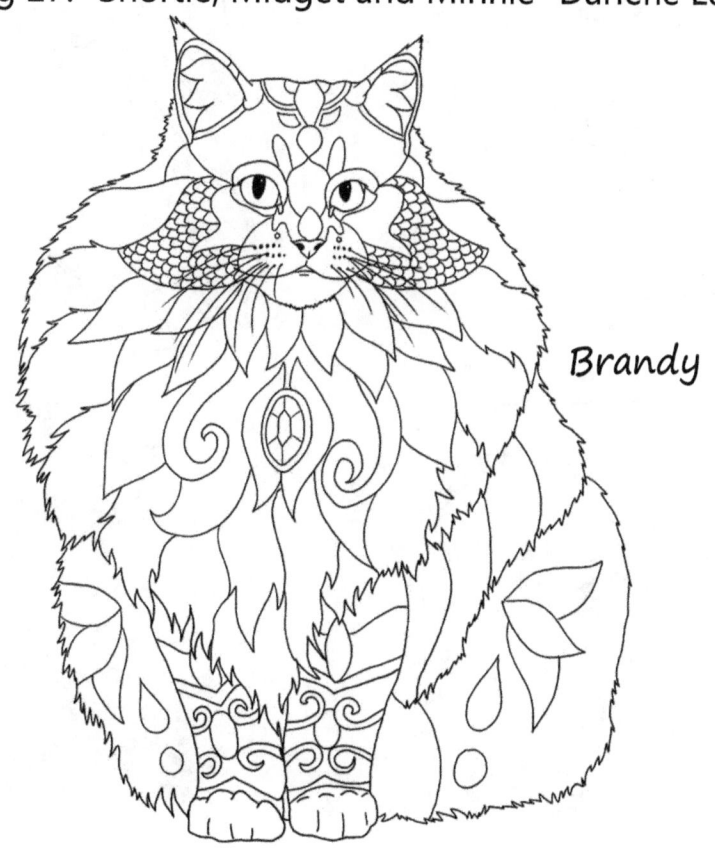

Brandy

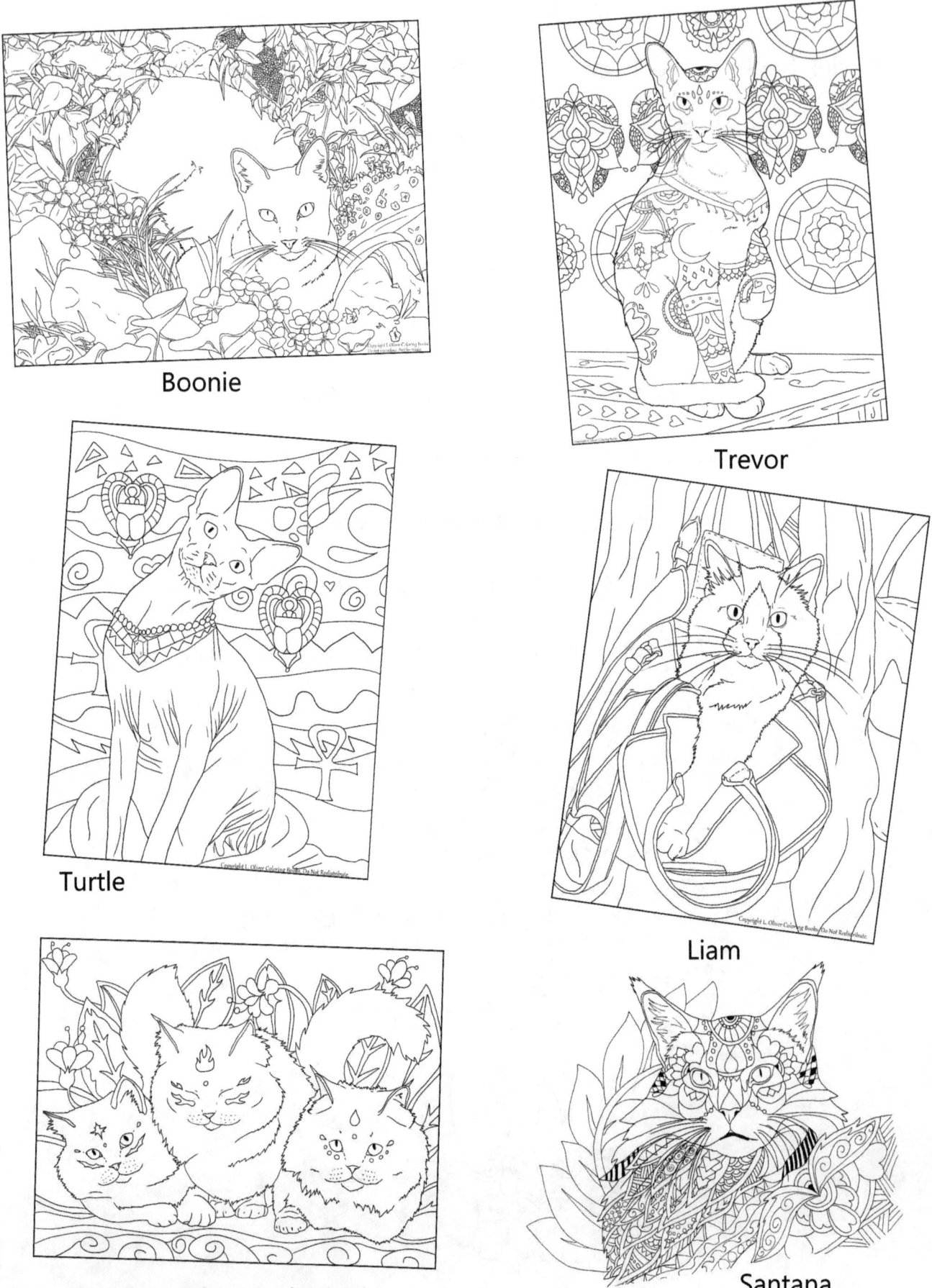

Boonie

Trevor

Turtle

Liam

Shortie, Midget and Minnie

Santana